1620

Recollets build Notre-Dame-des-Anges chapel at Quebec.

1621
Privy Council charters William Alexander as proprietor of New Scotland (Nova Scotia).

1622
Population at Quebec: 50.

Etienne Brûlé reaches Lake Superior.

1625
The first Jesuit missionaries arrive at Quebec.

First known métis child born to Micmac woman fathered by Charles de La Tour.

1627
Cardinal Richelieu forms the Company of the Hundred Associates to manage and colonize New France.

1628
British lay siege to starving Quebec. Champlain sent to England as prisoner.

First plow drawn by oxen used by Guillaumé Couillard.

First Scottish settlement established near Port-Royal.

1631
Thomas James and Luke Foxe explore James and Hudson Bays.

1632
First Jesuit *Relation* published in France to publicize missions.

1633
Champlain returns to Quebec; Brébeuf, Daniel and Jesuits take over Recollet missions.

1634
First seigneury of Beauport granted to Robert Giffard.

Jean Nicollet explores Lake Michigan region.

1635
Jesuit college and library founded at Quebec.

1636
Montmagny arrives as first governor of New France.

Fr. Gabriel Sagard publishes *L'histoire du Canada* with first Huron dictionary.

1638
Earthquake tremors recorded for six months, Montreal to Gaspé.

1639
Jesuits found the mission Saint Marie-among-the-Hurons on Georgian Bay.

Ursulines start convent school at Quebec.

Jesuits number Huron nation at c. 20,000 persons.

1640

First play (title unknown) acted at Quebec with Martial Piraube in lead role.

1642
Ville-Marie-de-Montréal founded by Maisonneuve.

Floods threaten Ville-Marie. Maisonneuve plants cross on Mont Réal when waters subside.

1643
Iroquois war spreads north. Ville-Marie lives under siege.

1644
Marguerite Bourgeoys obtains land grant for nuns of the Congrégation de Notre-Dame.

1645
Trade and colonizing rights tranferred to the Community of Habitants.

D'Aulnay-La Tour feud ends with sacking of Fort La Tour.

1646
Corneille's play *Le Cid* performed at Quebec.

1647
Council of New France formed.

1648
First white child, Barbe Meusnier, born in Montreal.

Jacques Brisson opens first licensed tavern in Quebec.

Iroquois-Huron war breaks out with renewed fury.

1649
Brébeuf and Lalément killed; Jesuits abandon Sainte-Marie.

First public execution: 16-year-old female thief.

1654
English expedition captures Fort La Tour and Acadia.

1657
First pendulum clock invented.

1658
Marguerite Bourgeoys opens first school in Montreal stable.

Date Due

Horwood, Harold Andrew
  Colonial Dream, 1497/1760

The Colonial Dream

FRANÇOIS GASTON DE LÉVIS BRIGADIER des ARMÉES du ROI de FRANCE
AU CANADA puis MARECHAL DE FRANCE, DUC de LÉVIS, CHEVALIER
DES ORDRES DU ROI GOUVERNEUR de la PROVINCE D'ARTOIS NÉ EN
1720 MORT EN 1787

The crowd that thronged the docks of Bristol in the spring of 1498 firmly believed that John Cabot and his son were headed for the riches of the Orient. The year before, the Italian navigator touched the coast of Newfoundland, which he judged to be an island near Cipango (Japan) or Cathay (China).

Previous page: *Gaston de Lévis took command of French forces after Montcalm's death. Gossips knew him as the man who stole the Intendant's mistress.*

Harold Horwood
The Colonial Dream
1497/1760

Canada's Illustrated Heritage

Canada's Illustrated Heritage

Publisher: Jack McClelland
Editorial Consultant: Pierre Berton
Historical Consultant: Michael Bliss
Editor-in-Chief: Toivo Kiil
Associate Editors: Michael Clugston
Clare McKeon
Harold Quinn
Jean Stinson
Assistant Editor: Marta Howard
Design: William Hindle
Lynn Campbell
Neil Fraser Cochrane
Cover Artist: Alan Daniel
Picture Research: Lembi Buchanan
Michel Doyon
Betty Gibson
Christine Jensen
Margot Sainsbury

ISBN: 0-9196-4414-7

N.S.L. Natural Science of Canada Limited
254 Bartley Drive
Toronto, Ontario M4A 1G1

Printed and bound in Canada

First it was the lure of gold, jewels, silks and spices of China, then
the rich fishing stocks of the Grand Banks, but finally it was the
beaver pelt that brought the Europeans to Canada. This preposterous
view of a beaver hunt (probably based on hearsay) was printed in 1715.

Contents

Navigators in the 16th century were no longer afraid of sailing off the end of the world, but the oceans were still strange and terrifying expanses. Surrounded by fantastical monsters, mythological goddesses and gods, mermaids, and an enormous bird carrying away an elephant (right), the navigator tries to fix his position.

New Found Lands

Be it known and made manifest that we have given and granted . . . to our beloved John Cabot full and free authority, faculty and power to sail to all parts, regions and coasts of the eastern, western and northern sea, under our banners, flags and ensigns. . . .

Henry VII of England, March 5, 1496

When Europeans discovered what we now call Canada in the fifteenth and sixteenth centuries, the Norse voyages to Markland and Vinland had been all but forgotten, and the new land–discovered by the English, but explored mostly by the French– was hardly greeted with enthusiasm; rather it was regarded as a geographical nuisance barring the way to China. Neither Cabot nor Cartier nor any explorer in the years between had much interest in the land itself. Only the fish merchants of Bristol and Saint-Malo had the wit to see that the discovery might be valuable for its own sake. Kings and courtiers and "gentlemen adventurers" continued to hope to get around it or across it in one way or another so that they could lay hands on the fabled wealth of the East.

Even the early colonies–all of which failed– were intended as collecting stations for silks and spices. Not till the nineteenth century did a pound of Canadian silver fox fetch ten times the price of a pound of silk. When New France was founded, fur was still mainly a raw material for hats, and most fur-trading companies went bankrupt while companies trading to India and China piled up vast wealth.

It all began with the Renaissance, the overpowering ferment that produced Leonardo da Vinci, Shakespeare, and Vasco da Gama. And *that* began with the Crusades, Christendom's ill-conceived effort to establish the Kingdom of God by bloodshed. As wars of conquest the Crusades failed miserably, but they revealed to medieval Europe vast worlds of knowledge hidden from the Church Fathers.

Only thirty-nine years after the fall of Constantinople to the Turks, Columbus sailed west with a crusader's cross embroidered on his shirt. Thirty years later, Magellan's expedition returned from the first voyage around the world. Between these two events the fishermen of England, France and Portugal had founded in eastern Canada one of the greatest fishing enterprises in human history.

For the first eighty years of the sixteenth century, fur trading was just a minor activity of the fishermen. They traded with Indians when they happened to come into contact with them. Fur was still a by-product of meat hunting. But as the Indians discovered the European demand for furs, they began trapping animals especially for their skins, producing more and more fur, and of better quality. By 1581, the French merchants of Saint-Malo, Rouen and Dieppe were fitting out ships es-

The first known European to reach North America was the Viking, Bjarni Herjolfsson in the year 986. On his way from Iceland to Greenland, he and his oarsmen (numbering about 30) were blown off course and reached the coast probably south of Nova Scotia. Some fifteen years later, another Viking, Leif Eiriksson, and some of Herjolfsson's crew landed somewhere to the south of the St. Lawrence and named the new land Vinland. In 1893, a replica of their boat with a crew of 32 sailed from Norway to Newfoundland in a mere 28 days.

The first accounts of Atlantic crossings occur in the Celtic legends dating as far back as the year 725, when Irish monks reached the east coast of Iceland.
Legend has it that St. Brendan, seen here saying Mass on what he thought was an island, made two voyages in search of "The Land of Promise" as early as AD 500.

pecially to trade for furs up the St. Lawrence. Economically the fur trade remained inferior to the fishery and never employed a tenth as many Europeans, but it opened up the continent to exploration, which the fishery did not, and it converted the hunting Indian tribes of eastern Canada into tribes of traders, making them dependent upon the white man.

The people who manned the ships for the Cabots and Corte-Reals, and caught and cured the fish for the merchants of Bristol and Saint-Malo, were wholly untouched by the great awakening that drove their masters to the remote corners of the earth. They remained in the Middle Ages, living within a narrow set of rites and superstitions, in a world where life and death were ruled by the caprice of gods and devils. They lived, often briefly and violently, and worked in conditions that we would think intolerable, but they had their joys and pleasures just the same. They brought them to this land and planted them here – their games, their music, their dances and songs – and in the freedom of the wilderness, these blossomed into the rich folk culture that survives in Newfoundland and Quebec.

Looking back at early Canada, we see some outstanding men and a few women, often aristocrats, sometimes wealthy, clothed in royal prerogatives, carrying charters from the courts of kings. But if we look more closely, we also catch glimpses of other men and women who populated the country – the colonists who died of scurvy under Roberval; the pickpockets and cutpurses reprieved from French galleys and sent out as labourers for priests and nuns and traders; the "King's girls" who became pioneer housewives for men they did not know in a land they could only imagine was something like France; the hordes of pirates and smugglers who ran a more successful fur trade than the royal monopolists; and the "masterless men" who lived like the Indians.

9

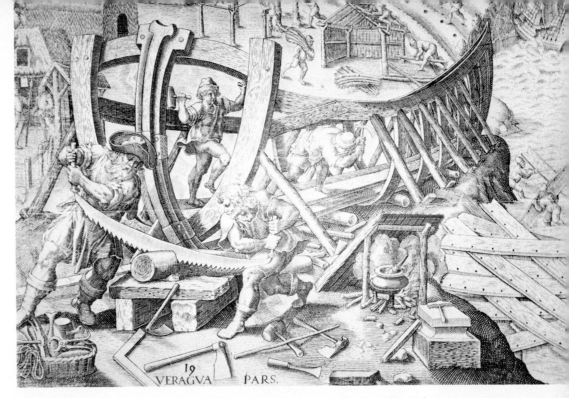

Shipwrecks on the high seas and in uncharted coastal waters of the New World kept carpenters busy with repairs. Above, they rebuild a caravel using broadaxes, adzes, mallets, pegs and pitch, while crewmen put up a makeshift shelter. Below, shipwrights and blacksmiths accompanying Martin Frobisher on his 1578 expedition repair ships damaged by ice floes west of Baffin Island.

Clothed in the high fashion of the court of Louis XIV, René-Robert Cavelier (known in history books as La Salle) accepts the King's commission to explore the western reaches of New France. Three years later in 1687, hopelessly lost on the Gulf of Mexico, he was murdered by an associate.

Americans, glamourizing their past, like to think there was a great rush to the New World soon after the Pilgrims landed at Plymouth Rock. They see the downtrodden masses of Europe scampering across the Atlantic seeking freedom. Nothing of the kind happened. All the early colonizing companies went bankrupt, whether their grants were in Nova Scotia, Newfoundland or Quebec, and one of their great problems was simple lack of bodies. The famous Company of One Hundred had more shareholders in France than it had colonists in Canada. When Jeanne Mance, a Frenchwoman from the professional classes, decided in 1640 to come to Canada to found a hospital, she was regarded in Paris as a voluntary martyr, going to lay down her life among the savages for the glory of God and King.

Only in the remote fishing stations and on the trails of the fur trade was there anything resembling freedom in early Canada. The official colonies—Port Royal, Cupids, Ferryland, Quebec and all the others—were little models of European society, absolute monarchies on a small scale. The social gulf was extreme. There were gentlemen and ladies . . . and others. The whole social order consisted of making the "others" perform their proper functions of supporting and serving the handful of privileged people, the ones with the charters and the deeds and the prerogatives.

Every town and village had its whipping post (the little settlement of Ferryland had three), but it would be wrong to think of the social order as a reign of terror. People accepted the stratified society and the assumption that the masterless man was an outlaw. At first there were no prisons, no full-time police, no organized system of justice. Just a common-sense order enforced by property owners and confined to the village limits. Governors and intendants and fishing admirals enforced the law after a fashion, without necessarily having any legal training. Upper-class wrongdoers might be fined. Lower-class offenders without money could only be hanged, pilloried, flogged or banished. The last of these sentences, called "transportation," was a sale into temporary or permanent slavery in Virginia or the West Indies, where forced labour was needed. And whether in fact it was any better than death is debatable.

While all this was going on, the freebooters were creating a sort of parallel society, and in some senses laying the basis for modern Canada. Men who had sailed under pirate flags, (as five thousand Newfoundland fishermen were reported to have done in the seventeenth century), or had lived illegally as *coureurs de bois* in the wilderness or as masterless men in forest villages, were not easily awed by wigs and ribbons and lace cuffs. A spirit of independence affected even the settlements. Practically the entire colony of New France connived to protect the five hundred outlawed *coureurs de bois* from the reach of French law. The masterless men patterned their lives consciously on the Indians, and perhaps learned from them that men and women could govern themselves by consensus, rather than being ruled by divine right. Thousands of Acadian farmers, too, managed to

govern themselves with no authority higher than the village meeting (presided over by the parish priest), and on this basis built a stable society that persisted for almost a century.

At the same time war was the normal way of life. Even fishing ships in our first three centuries were armed with cannon. Early settlers fought the Dutch, fought the Indians, fought the pirates, fought each other in a series of English-French wars that lasted for a hundred years, and finally fought the Americans. It is now hard for us to imagine a time when most men and many women were part-time soldiers, always ready to repel an invasion, but that is the way they lived and raised their children, enjoying few moments of security.

The character of Canada was formed in those early centuries, and unlike the people of safe and settled New England, the first European settlers were always a minority, always facing odds of greater strength and greater numbers, always pitted against the wilderness, against enemies, against foreign exploiters, but all the more determined to build island societies that would be safe and conservative and well-governed, and in the end, perhaps even peaceful.

Although the Jesuit "Blackrobes" met with little success in their efforts to convert the Indians to Christianity, their accounts are a fascinating, if often biased, record of everyday life in early New France. This history of Canada by François du Creux was published in 1664.

Gallows, stocks and pillories were among the first structures erected in village squares – instruments of this Old World system of justice. There were no lawyers in New France, and according to the statutes, a person could be hanged for rape, pilloried for being poor or drunk, and have his tongue cut out for blasphemy.

Over a year before Columbus, on his third voyage, came in sight of the mainland, John Cabot planted the flag of Henry VII of England somewhere between Labrador and Cape Breton. A second voyage southward along the Atlantic Coast a year later (1498) ended "talk of Asia lying on the other side of the Ocean."

CHAPTER ONE

The Island of Brasil

It is considered certain that the cape of the said land was found and discovered in the past by the men from Bristol who found "Brasil" as your Lordship well knows . . . and it is assumed and believed to be the mainland. . . .

Letter from John Day to Columbus, 1497

Fifteenth-century Europe had forgotten the New World. The legend of Vinland survived only in Iceland and in the archives of the Vatican. Markland, to which Greenlanders were making voyages at least as late as the mid-fourteenth century, was perhaps known vaguely, but if so it was assumed to be an island somewhere in the northwest.

Meanwhile European fishermen were voyaging far to the west, especially from the English port of Bristol. Since the twelfth century the Bristol merchants had been trading north and south. The fleece of Cotswold sheep was woven in Bristol into woollen goods that were then exported in Bristol-built ships to Iceland, Spain and Portugal. From Spain and Portugal they brought back wine (sherry was called "Bristol milk"), and from Iceland stockfish (dried cod). After a time they decided to catch the Iceland cod themselves: as early as 1412, Bristol crews were fishing Icelandic waters and wintering there. Icelandic records show as many as thirty ships engaged in this trade, but it was a precarious one, depending on the whims of Scandinavian kings. By the 1470s, English rights in

Iceland were subject to constant negotiation and bickering, and Bristol firms were searching for alternative fishing grounds.

There was a legendary island called "Brasil" or "Hy-Brasil." (The similarity of the name to "Brazil" – called after a tropical tree that yields a red dye – is a coincidence that has confused writers on the discovery of the Americas for five centuries.) Hy-Brasil is in Irish mythology the Isle of the Blest, and it is said to appear off the west coast of Ireland every seven years. (The last recorded sighting was by a Professor Westropp in 1872.) The practical and literal-minded Bristol merchants, needing a new fishing base, determined to pin down this elusive bit of land.

In 1480, a merchant named John Jay the Younger sent out a vessel under Captain Thomas Lloyd to find Brasil. After three months he returned, unsuccessful. But even though he did not reach land, he may have got as far as the fishing banks, because the next year Thomas Croft, collector of customs at Bristol, sent two ships, the *George* and the *Trinitie*, to the western Atlantic, each, according to the exchequer account, carrying forty bushels of fishery salt. The account also states that the ships intended to "search and find a certain Ile called the Isle of Brasile."

They were persistent about it. In 1498, Pedro de Ayala, the Spanish ambassador in London, reporting to the King on Cabot's discovery of New-

This 1493 engraving made in Spain illustrated Columbus' official account of his first voyage. The ship, supposedly a replica of the Santa Maria, was built along the lines of the unwieldy Portuguese caravels. Within a few years, most navigators were rigging their ships with the more manoeuverable lateen (or triangular) sails of the Arabs, and ships were built longer and sleeker.

Almost all the accounts of the early voyages to Canada, including those of Cabot, record that waters around Newfoundland and Labrador were teeming with fish. For centuries Eskimo and Indian tribes of the region, dressed in sealskins, had fished there, and by the 1500s, Portuguese, Basque and English fishermen were making excursions of four thousand miles for the catch.

foundland, said: "For the last seven years the people of Bristol have equipped two, three, four caravels to go in search of the Island of Brasil and the Seven Cities." (The latter was another legendary island, later associated with Nova Scotia.) It seems unlikely that these hardheaded merchants would have kept on doing this with nothing to show for it; but if they had at least reached the Grand Banks, they would have been able to make the voyages pay by bringing back plenty of fish.

the way to Cathay

Did they also find land? There is one piece of evidence that they did. John Day, the English merchant then living in Spain, described John Cabot's voyage of 1497 in a letter to "the Lord Great Admiral" (almost certainly Columbus) and said:

It is considered certain that this same point of land at another time was found and discovered by those of Bristol who found el Brasil as you are already aware.

But Day, who had been a wine-importer in Bristol in 1492-3, had perhaps been too credulous in listening to sailors boasting in a dockside tavern. It would be surprising if the shrewd and careful Henry VII of England would have commissioned an Italian to do what his own subjects had already done, and then rewarded him for doing it. All the same, it remains possible. And if it is true, it detracts little from John Cabot's achievement, for the new thing that he pursued was not merely a bit of land; it was a way to Cathay, a dream and a passion born from gazing at a sphere upon whose surface he had etched the uncertain outlines of land and sea.

This silk-clad dandy who stood by the docks of Bristol directing preparations for a voyage of exploration in the year 1496 was a true Renaissance man, citizen of the world, far travelled and well read. He held citizenship in the Republic of Ven-

14

ice, but was probably a native of Genoa. He had trod the sands of Mecca and seen the caravans of silks and spices coming over the road from Xanadu. Like Columbus, he was one of the new breed whose thoughts and plans encompassed not Europe but the world.

Cabot knew as much as any man of the interlocked spheres of earth and heavens. He had dangled their images before the crowned heads of Europe—globes and charts of his own making, showing how the world narrowed toward the poles and the Far East came close to England. Not one of his maps or globes has survived—they went into dustbins during the centuries when Cabot himself was forgotten and his voyages to the New World, only half-remembered, were credited to his son Sebastian.

Cabot had landed at Bristol in 1495, ten years after King Henry VII had brought the Wars of the Roses to an end. For the first time in a century, the country had stable government, though it was fretting under Henry's heavy taxation. Wages were the highest in history: a penny a day, sometimes as much as two pennies—enough to purchase four pounds of fresh beef or mutton, though in Bristol dried codfish was the big item in the food trade.

a greater mart than Venice

In a sense, it was fish that had brought Cabot to Bristol, for in pursuit of fish the Bristol seamen were already roving northern waters from Norway to Iceland, and probably, as we have seen, to the Grand Banks. Perhaps this shallow part of the sea was just off the Asian continent, with the fabled cities of silks and jewels and spices just a little way beyond? He went around telling everyone that England could corner this trade and become "a greater mart than Venice."

The tight-fisted king, who had piled up great wealth in the ten years of his reign, leapt at the

If this elaborate 19th century engraving had lived up to its title, "Portraits of men connected with the discovery of America," the page would be filled with well over three hundred portraits. Some say the Paleo-Indians were the discoverers, crossing the Alaskan land bridge 40,000 years ago. Others say the Vikings, or Irish monks. Americans claim Columbus, Canadians Cabot.

15

A 1578 tally of vessels off the coast of the New Found Land reads "over 100 saile of Spaniards . . . 20 or 30 from Biskaie . . . of Portugals above 50 . . . of the French nation and the Britons about 150." The fish they were catching was mostly cod, prepared in two ways: the "green-cod" method of cleaning, salting and pressing the fish into barrels; and the English "dry-cod" method above. The catch here is cleaned on covered "stages," then spread on "flakes" to dry.

chance to corner the spice trade by the inexpensive gamble of backing Cabot's voyage. He granted a charter giving Cabot the right to conquer and occupy heathen lands, with a monopoly on the trade, and access to all the free convict labour he might need.

fair winds all the way

So Cabot bought a ship, hired Bristol pilots and crew, and set off in the summer of 1496 to locate the mainland of Asia. This voyage failed. He had started too late in the year, when westerlies are almost continuous, and these drove him back to Ireland. Next year he tried again, starting in May, and had fair winds from the east and northeast, nearly all the way.

By now he had a fine ship, the *Mathew*, fifty tons – not considered small at that time. She seems to have been built for the job, and the name *Mathew* is probably an anglicization of Mattea, Cabot's wife. To modern eyes the ship would look rather like a tub, but a very seaworthy one. She bore no resemblance to those top-heavy floating castles beloved in Spain. Her deck was wide and level, right to the bow, which was broad and blunt. A low quarter-deck, rising only five or six feet, covered the stern, but overall she was flat and barge-like. Beamy, deep and round-bellied, she could weather almost any storm, but she must have been slow and unhandy in contrary winds.

Her eighteen men lived belowdecks in crowded conditions, but in the fifteenth century it was not uncommon for ships of her size to carry fifty people – insurance against deaths from fever, scurvy and plague. Crewmen slept on wooden bunks in tiers about two feet apart, or found what space they could among the cargo. Ships lightly manned sometimes found themselves without crews, and on one English voyage to Norway, every soul from captain to cabin boy died of the Black Death.

No firsthand account of the second Cabot voyage survives; none of the accounts we have – all written by landsmen – make complete geographical sense. Guesses at Cabot's first landfall range from northern Newfoundland to Maine, taking in Cape Bonavista, Cape Spear, Cape Race and Cape Breton on the way. But the landfall is important only to people who want to erect monuments for tourists. Cabot's discovery was something else. He had located a coast that appeared to be mainland – not a mere island. This could only be the coast of Asia, with its silks and spices a short distance further south!

Cabot returned to Bristol August 6, 1497, and promptly became a popular idol, chased about by crowds. He had made the voyage back from the northeast cape of "Cathay" in fifteen days, and was already conferring titles on friends who would accompany him next year. They would be counts or barons in the new land. A priest from Venice was to be its first bishop. Cabot himself was already regarded as its prince, royal vassal to Henry.

velvet, silks and feathers

He made the most of his fame. A conspicuous dresser, he strutted about London in velvet, silks and feathers. Men's dress at the time was absurdly top-heavy. Gorgeous doublets, slashed at the sleeve, revealed colourful silk underclothes. A velvet mini-cloak might also be worn, and a flat hat with sweeping plumes. All this finery came barely to the waist. Below it, a padded and decorated cod-piece lied about the gentleman's sexual equipment, just as the padded bra lied about the American bust four and a half centuries later. Except for this jewelled protuberance, the more extreme dandies went nude from hip to ankle, but Cabot probably preferred to display his wealth in skin-tight silk panty-hose. Such colours as fuchsia and prim-

**Sebastian Cabot
The Great Talker**

For over 300 years, historians and mapmakers believed his stories, but as a boy of 13, it is unlikely that Sebastian Cabot had anything to do with his father John's discoveries. He probably did lead an expedition to Hudson Bay in 1508 – at least he *claimed* to have found the elusive Northwest Passage. In 1527, on a Spanish expedition to the East by way of Cape Horn, he stopped to look for gold on Argentina's Rio de la Plata. His officers objected and were marooned. Back in Spain, he was sentenced to three years exile in Africa, but talked his way out of the sentence. Employed by Spain and England, he secretly tried to sell his services to the Council of Ten in Venice, and in 1544 tried to add substance to his claims by publishing a world map. He died in 1557, still talking.

The Cross-Staff

In order to find how far north or south he was, an up-to-date sailor in the 1600s no longer consulted his astrolabe or star chart if he had a cross-staff. By moving the sliding cross-piece along a scale, he set up the angle between the horizon (B) and the sun (C) with his eye (A), and read his latitude. But despite its accuracy compared to the astrolabe, the cross-staff had two problems: under overcast skies it was useless, and in bright sunlight "shooting the sun" caused severe damage to the eyes.

rose were favoured. Flat, broad-toed shoes of velvet completed the costume.

So attired, he was received at court and offered command of a new expedition, fitted out for both colonization and trade with as many as ten ships and "all the malefactors in the kingdom" to be transported for forced labour.

This "colony" was to be a trading station, a place where ships could refit and reprovision on voyages between England and tropical Asia, and where cargoes could be stored for trans-shipment. The intention was to build a manned fort, perhaps in Newfoundland or Nova Scotia, like the "factories" later built by the Hudson's Bay Company, but more elaborate.

Cabot started in the spring of 1498 with five ships, not ten. He had with him, however, not only common sailors and malefactors to the number of about three hundred, but also merchants and clerics, including Italian friars and a priest named Antonio de Carbonaris, the "bishop" for whom Carbonear on Newfoundland's east coast is probably named.

gala departure

It was a gala departure, with flags and bunting and a whole company of gentlemen adventurers strutting on quarter decks in silk and velvet. The common tars (not to mention the malefactors, stored out of sight or chained below) enjoyed no such finery. A pair of coarse woollen pants might be their only garment. They went barefooted and bareheaded, but some of them, at least, owned a kind of hooded woollen shirt for use in bad weather. Waterproof clothes had not yet been invented, but a type of apron coated with tar was sometimes worn. Hair was either cropped or tied at the nape of the neck. Gentlemen wore it very long, in the style known in the twentieth century as the "pageboy." There was thus an extreme contrast between

the working man and gentleman: they looked – and acted – like creatures of separate species.

The middle class that was to dominate the world three centuries later was just then beginning to emerge: shipowners and traders who were not gentlemen but also not the "scum" who swabbed decks, carried out the gentlemen's slops, lived on hard tack and water and a little salt fish, and died of scurvy in the forward hold. These men of substance, if not of family, tended to survive their voyages, drive successful bargains, grow wealthy, and live to a ripe age.

an astonishing silence

The plan of the voyage was to sail to the New Found Land, then coast southwestward to the tropics, founding a suitable colony in a place not occupied by a civilized nation, then going on to the cities of China, and perhaps to the spice-growing lands that Cabot knew lay southwest from the dominions of the Great Khan. Trouble developed early when one of the ships – probably Cabot's, though this isn't certain – was so mauled by a storm that she had to put back to Ireland for repairs. After that there is an astonishing silence. The voyage is not mentioned again in the records of Bristol, London or the international correspondence. What happened to the colonists, the priests, the traders and merchants who set out so confidently for Canada in the spring of 1498 with provisions for a full year? We don't know. We only know that Cabot's pension was paid by the King in 1499. After that, total silence.

That this massive venture should have drawn a blank is not surprising. The expedition, doomed from the start, must have proven that the new land was not the coast of Asia but a wild continent, inhabited by "savages." Still worse, if Cabot coasted all the way to South America, as some maps suggest, he must have discovered that there was no

Sailing by the Stars

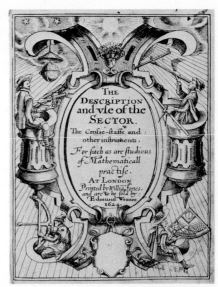

In the 16th and 17th centuries, sailing was more or less a "by guess and by god" business. There were navigational instruments, of course, but since all of these depended on sighting positions of the sun and the horizon, and the stars at night, the pitch-and-roll of high seas usually made the measurements go haywire. The astrolabe (seen below in one of its variants) was the oldest of these devices – an adaptation of the sundial that could be used to tell time and give the ship's latitude. By 1624, the cross-staff, the quadrant, the sector and the globe (seen clockwise in Edmund Weaver's ad at right) had taken some of the guess-work out of navigation, but it would take another century and the invention of the sextant before sailing became anything close to a science. The first compasses were crude devices too – magnetized needles floating on water or hanging by a thread. And maps? Which could be trusted? Most were based on logs and second-hand accounts. Better to sail by the stars and dead reckoning.

Sailors' instruments sold in 1624.

By sighting the sun, this explorer used the astrolabe to tell time and read latitude. The first accurate measurements of longitude weren't made until the 1790s.

way past it. English and Portuguese navigators, both separately and together, promptly turned their interest to the Northwest Passage.

the Bristol Company

As far as Canada was concerned, the fishery was well-known and well-established, and the Bristol merchants realized that other kinds of wealth also might be extracted from the New Found Land. They organized the Bristol Company of Adventurers, with a patent issued in 1502, and tried to found a colony in 1503. Again we have only a few clues to what happened. Some of the Bristol merchants went on long voyages and spent winters away from their home port. Thomas Ashenhurst, for example, was an active trader of the time, but his name is absent from the Bristol records of 1503 right through the following winter and summer until August 1504. Then he resumed trading. That same year Hugh Eliot, William Clerk and William Thorne are absent from the records through the spring and summer until August. All these men were members of the Bristol Company. It seems likely that they did plant a colony at Newfoundland in 1503 as they intended, and that Ashenhurst stayed with the colony over winter and returned with Thorne, Eliot and Clerk when they made another voyage in 1504.

But again the evidence ends in silence. The company petered out, with some of its principals suing one another for unpaid debts. At the same time the fishery flourished, and the harbours of Newfoundland and Cape Breton were gradually built up with stores and stages and houses. St. John's became a free port, where the ships of England, Portugal, France and later Spain forgathered every summer for fishing and barter.

Though there may have been a small fishery on the banks before Cabot, and the Basques may have reached Labrador by way of Greenland even earlier, the publicity of the voyage of 1497 created a rush to Newfoundland. The Portuguese were on the coast by 1501, and the French by 1504. By 1508, Newfoundland fish was a common article in both France and England.

The first surviving letter sent from Canada to Europe is addressed to King Henry VIII by a shipmaster named John Rut and dated "In the haven of St. John the third day of August written in haste 1527." Rut had coasted Labrador looking for a northwest passage, then fished in the Strait of Belle Isle, then called at St. John's, where he found "Eleven saile of Normans and one Brittaine and two Portugal barques all a fishing." During the same decade, the Portuguese tried to found a colony on Cape Breton Island, but little is known about it, not even its exact site. By mid-century they were sending a hundred and fifty ships to Newfoundland each summer, but the Spanish Basque fleet was even larger: in round figures, two hundred ships with six thousand men.

frozen in harbour

Throughout the sixteenth century (and even later), Europeans often died of scurvy when they tried to winter in Canada. The worst disaster of the kind happened in 1577, when the Basque fleet was unexpectedly frozen into harbour in the Strait of Belle Isle, forcing the men to winter there. Despite limitless supplies of fish and oil, five hundred and forty of them died.

But some winter crews were left by the English, and these in time became permanent settlers. When Jacques Cartier made his first exploring voyage, all major ports from Canso, Nova Scotia, to southern Labrador were well known, and St. John's had facilities for repairing and servicing ships and gear.

Telling Time

Before the first pocket watches and pendulum clocks were invented in the mid-17th century, telling time, especially at night, was a complicated problem. Astrolabes and nocturnals (above) calculated time by the relative positions of the sun and stars, but most seafaring adventurers kept time with a sand-glass. In John Cabot's time, it was the duty of the crewman "on watch" to call out when the last grain of sand fell into the bottom glass, and then reverse it promptly. Falling asleep on the job or "warming the glass" (thereby increasing the opening and flow of sand) were punishable offences.

Terra Incognita

Before Cabot and his contemporaries returned from their voyages, the Atlantic – the Sea of Darkness – marked the western boundary of the habitable world for most Europeans. Although the Vinland Map of 1440 shows an island that is almost certainly Newfoundland, all other charts of the North Atlantic end at Greenland – *ultimus terre terminus,* the furthest land known.

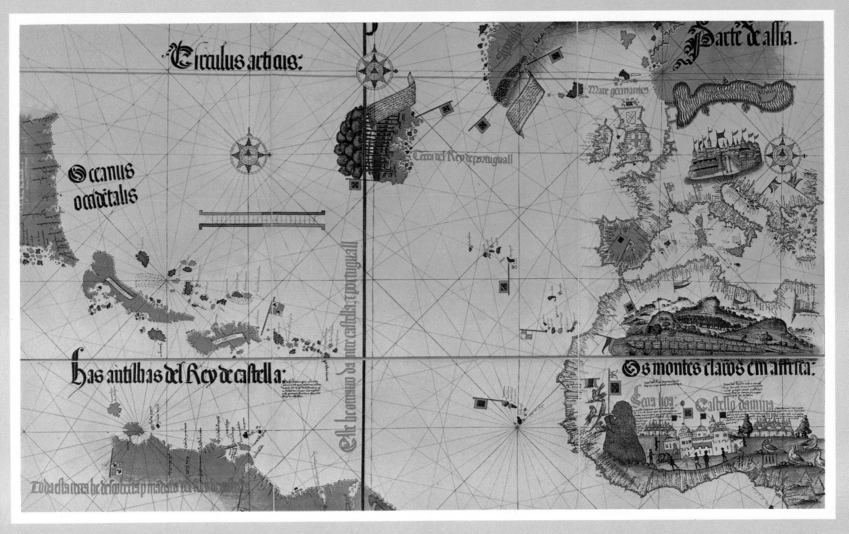

To make sense out of the 1502 Cantino map, Newfoundland is shown as an island (top centre) and the coast of Florida as the land mass on the left-hand edge.

Mapmakers' Follies

Canada first appeared on a map around 1500 as a jut of land presumed to be the northeast coast of China. It made sense. To geographers of the time the earth was one-quarter smaller. As explorers returned with new charts, place names crowded out illustrations and the continent seemed to grow, along with the exaggerated claims of explorers, kings and their mapmakers.

Jacques Cartier's arrival in Canada is included in detail in this illustration from the Vallard Atlas of 1547. To read the map properly the book should be turned upside down, thus showing Cartier's group (standing on their heads) on the north shore of the Rio do Canadas.

Nicholas de Fer's map of Nouvelle-France (1718) shows the route taken by La Salle across the Great Lakes and down the Mississippi in 1685. Many of the details of this and other maps were added to give the impression that explorers had claimed lands they actually had never seen.

A native draped in a fleur de lis *mantle kneels before one of the two "paintings-within-the-painting" of the patron saints of New France. The large canvas, one of the first paintings done in Canada and titled* La France apportant la foi aux Indiens de la Nouvelle-France *(c. 1671), is attributed to the missionary, Frère Luc.*

CHAPTER TWO

The Kingdom of the Saguenay

We have found stones like Diamants, the most faire, pollished and excellently cut that it is possible for a man to see. When the Sunne shineth upon them, they glister as it were sparkles of fire.

Hakluyt account of Cartier's Voyages, 1541-43

When Jacques Cartier was commissioned by the King of France to find a short route to Asia, the New Found Land of the fishermen was still believed to be a collection of islands, with the Pacific Ocean only a few miles to the west. He was to find a way past those islands, claim whatever mineral wealth they might contain, and then sail on to China.

Cartier and his men – some of them criminals, but all sworn into the King's service – sailed in two ships from his home port, Saint-Malo, on April 20, 1534, and arrived at Catalina, Newfoundland, on May 10. Eleven days later they sailed to Funk Island for a load of birds. Cartier wrote:

Some of these birds are as large as geese, being black and white with a beak like a crow. They are always in the water, being unable to fly, since they have tiny wings about half the size of your hand, with which, however, they can move through the water as rapidly as other birds through the air. These birds are marvellously fat. We call them Apponatz, and in less than half an hour our longboats were log-loaded with

them. *Each of our ships salted four or five casks, not to mention those we ate fresh.*

These great auks, looking like overgrown penguins, were used by all fishermen of the French shore before and after Cartier's time for meat and oil and as bait for fishing lines, until the last great auk was killed in 1844.

On Wednesday May 27 we reached the entrance to Castle Bay [Strait of Belle Isle] but because of bad weather and the numerous icebergs we encountered we stopped at Quirpon, where we remained, unable to leave, until June 9, when we departed, to continue with God's help.

They sailed southward through the Strait to Bonne Espérance, then called Brest. In Cartier's time, and for many years thereafter, Brest was the principal rendezvous for the French and French Basques fishing and whaling in the Strait of Belle Isle and along southern Labrador. It was so much frequented that it gave rise to the legend of "the City of Brest" in New France, which French writers of the seventeenth century believed to be a metropolis as large and populous as a European city. Here they landed, said Mass, and replenished their supplies. Forty or fifty miles to the south, still on the north shore of the Gulf of St. Lawrence, they met a large fishing vessel that had lost its way. They directed it back to Brest. Soon afterwards

This strange and fanciful drawing of Jacques Cartier was published in the Codex Canadensis *around the year 1700, over 150 years after his death. The artist is thought to be the defrocked Jesuit missionary, Louis Nicholas. Only two sketches of Cartier from his own time have survived: one on a 1542 map by Pierre Desceliers, the second in the Vallard Atlas of 1547 (page 22).*

they met their first Indians – seal hunters in birch-bark canoes. Then they crossed the Gulf and explored the full length of Newfoundland's west coast.

At the Magdalen Islands where they stopped, there were "many great beasts like big cows, which have two tusks in their jaws like elephant tusks, and swim about in the water. There was one asleep on the beach, and we set out in our longboats to try to catch it, but as soon as we approached, it cast itself into the sea."

persistent Indians

At Baie des Chaleurs, which they thought at first might be the wished-for strait to Asia, they met forty or fifty canoes full of people wanting to trade. "And seeing that no matter how much we made signs to them they would not retreat, we shot off over their heads two small cannon." This frightened them off, but only momentarily, "and when they came alongside our longboat we set off two fire lances which discharged among them and frightened them so much that they paddled away in great haste." No wonder. A fire lance was a primitive flame thrower packed with gunpowder, broken glass, bent nails and the like.

The persistent Indians returned next day and induced the French to trade. "We sent two men ashore to offer them some knives and other iron-ware and a red hat to give their captain . . . . They bartered everything they had to the point where they went away naked without a scrap of clothing, making signs that they would return next day with more pelts."

To those first Indians encountered by Cartier in the Gulf of St. Lawrence, Europeans were not complete strangers. They already knew what white men wanted from them. They held up beaver skins, offering to trade, and carefully hid away their women and girls. Whites were a clear danger (especially to women), but also a source of rare foreign weapons, cloth and ornaments.

Some of the first Indian slaves taken to Portugal in 1501 by the Corte-Real expedition of that year were already wearing bits of European jewelry, and one was carrying the hilt of a European sword. What contacts Indians had with Europeans before Cartier we do not really know, except that they must have been more extensive than the written records indicate.

Hunger for rare trinkets made dealing with whites well worth the danger. There is no support in documents of the time for the belief that the "simple savages" looked upon white men with wonder and awe. On the contrary, the Frenchmen who got to know the Indians best declared that the natives regarded themselves as superior to the French in every respect except in the possession of fine cloth, guns, and other hardware.

Cartier missed the entrance to the St. Lawrence River, thinking Anticosti part of the mainland, then coasted north and east along Labrador until he reached the Atlantic and headed home. Except for the two Indians there was little to show for the voyage – enough, however, to persuade the King to outfit a bigger expedition the next year.

a kingdom of vast wealth

When they returned to Canada in 1535, the two Indians could speak French well enough to explain that Anticosti was an island, with a great waterway behind it leading to kingdoms of vast wealth. To the Indians of the bleak Gaspé, the cultivated lands of the Iroquoians on the upper St. Lawrence *were* a kingdom of vast wealth. But to the French vast wealth meant jewels and gold and spices. Out of such Indian remarks and later stories, when they were perhaps told what they wanted to hear, the Europeans created the dream Kingdom of the Saguenay, somewhere along the

Almost all accounts of explorers' first impressions remark how little clothing the natives wore. "They go quite naked, except for a small skin and a few old furs . . ." Cartier described the Iroquois, "their heads shaved all round in circles, except for a tuft on the top of the head which they leave long like a horse's tail." (Quite a contrast to his own silk hose, slashed doublet and stylish "duck-bill" slippers!)

Cartier's obsession with the details of everyday life among the Indians left no activity unobserved: "We saw a large quantity of mackeral which they had caught near the shore with nets made of hemp-thread. Here also grows Indian corn like pease . . . which they eat in place of bread, and of this they had a large quantity."

27

The Founding of New France

"Show me, I pray you, the will of our father Adam, that I may see if he has really made you and the King of Portugal his universal heirs," wrote François I to the King of Spain in 1515. The letter was really a challenge, and nine years later France joined the contest for control of the New World. An expedition in 1524 along the East Coast found no passage to Mexico's gold or Cathay's silks and spices, and when its leader, Verrazzano, was eaten by cannibals in the Caribbean, François commissioned Jacques Cartier to explore a more northerly route and establish a toehold for France in Canada.

François I, decked out in silks and jewels, chartered Cartier "to discover lands where a great quantity of gold and precious things are to be found."

Jacques Cartier – the first to claim Canada for France. Before his commission in 1534, he lived a pirate's life, capturing and plundering Spanish vessels.

Even Hollywood's Cecil B. DeMille could not have trumped the pageantry that must have attended Cartier's return. He had crossed the Atlantic in 20 days, had not lost one of his 120 men, and even had two of Chief Donnacona's sons in tow. The courtiers' children in leopard skins may have been part of the theatrics.

Before hoisting the sails for the voyage home, Cartier raised a cross with the plaque Vive le Roi de la France *on the Gaspé shore. When the local chief protested, Cartier told him it was a marker for ships.*

St. Lawrence water system, and made repeated attempts to reach it.

Cartier's two captive Indians reported that the Saguenay was rich in red copper, and that it was only two days' sail from Anticosti. But this was forgotten or ignored in the lust to discover a new Mexico or Peru. The Indians actually pointed out the Saguenay River, but Cartier continued to seek it elsewhere, and indeed had reports of it much further to the west.

On this voyage Cartier wasted no time exploring the coast, but headed straight up the St. Lawrence to Île d'Orléans, and found a good harbour near what was then an Iroquoian village, Stadacona. Through his two captives he made friendly contact with their father, Donnacona, from whom he received further reports of the fabulous kingdom.

Cartier understood Donnacona to say that he had visited the Saguenay himself, that it held "infinite amounts of gold, rubies and other riches, and white men, as in France, dressed in woollen cloth."

It did not occur to the Frenchmen of the time that the Indian chief might be describing, at third or fourth hand, countries held by the Spaniards, far off to the south and west, but if the legends of the Kingdom of the Saguenay held any substance at all, then the lands of the Spanish conquest seem today to be the most likely explanation.

Cartier described Donnacona as *"le seigneur de Canada,"* thinking that this was the name of the country. In fact, *"canada"* must have meant simply "village," being close to the equivalent word in other Iroquoian languages. (The language of Donnacona's people, of which Cartier compiled an extensive vocabulary, is related to, but different from, the known Iroquoian tongues.)

30

Donnacona was anxious to keep the French from proceeding upriver to Hochelaga, and in an effort to cement a firm alliance with them, he gave Cartier three children: a ten-year-old girl and two younger boys, not as slaves but for adoption, following the custom of the Iroquoian peoples of cementing alliances by adoptions.

But Cartier insisted on going further, not realizing until much later that he was incurring the enmity of the people among whom he was already proposing to found a settlement. Leaving his ships at Stadacona, he continued upriver in boats. At the place later named the Richelieu Rapids, another chief presented Cartier with a child. They reached Hochelaga (which they now believed to be the gateway to the wealth of the Kingdom of the Saguenay) on October 2.

And on our arrival at Hochelaga more than a thousand people came out to meet us, men women and children giving us as great welcome as ever father gave to his son, making great signs of joy, for the men danced in one band, the women in another, and the children also, after which they brought stores of fish and of bread made from Indian corn, tossing so much of it into our longboats that it seemed to be raining bread . . . . And the women brought their children in arms to have them touched by the captain and the others who were with him.

It was fine land, with great fields of corn, which they use as we use wheat. And in the midst of the fields is the town of Hochelaga, at the foot of a mountain with cultivated slopes, from the top of which there is a great view, and we named this mountain Mount Royal.

The Iroquoian predecessor of Montreal was a walled town with only one gate and fifty long-

On his second voyage, Cartier set out for the Iroquois village of Hochelaga (now Montreal). After a cautious reception, the Indians brought him their sick to be cured. As in most historical paintings, many of the details in this 20th century reconstruction of Cartier's meeting are purely imaginative.

houses inside the palisade, each longhouse being thirty or forty feet wide and more than a hundred feet long. The total population was two to three thousand.

Barred from further progress by the Lachine Rapids, Cartier retreated to Stadacona and laid up his ships for the winter. The weather had been beautiful, and they expected nothing worse than the winters of western France.

dictates of fashion

Frenchmen of Cartier's time dressed in impractical doublet and hose. Doublets were usually sleeveless. Cloaks or capes rarely came below the hip, and the lower body was inadequately covered by a bloomer-like garment reaching only to mid-thigh and usually slashed into ribbons to satisfy the dictates of fashion. Even workingmen by now had forsaken the practical trousers of earlier times for their own version of this dress, in wool rather than silk or linen, and with hose that ended at the ankle, tied with a lace. (Since their shoes, when they wore any, were rough wooden clogs, hose with feet would soon have been in tatters.)

There was no waterproof footwear. Gentlemen wore cloth boots, almost useless in a Canadian winter. Peasants and sailors were somewhat better served by their clogs, but these were impractical in snow. Later colonists adopted the moccasins and snowshoes of the Indians, but Cartier's men did not.

They were appalled by the winter at Quebec, and totally unprepared. They watched in disbelief while the Indians, often wearing only loincloth and moccasins, walked across river ice on sunny days in February to visit the ships. The *sauvages* had no difficulty facing sub-zero days in near nudity, while the Frenchmen shivered in wet linen and wool, and wondered if they could last till spring. Many of them did not:

The sickness [scurvy] broke out among us with extreme and unusual symptoms, for some lost all their strength, their legs became swollen and inflamed, with sinews shrunken and black like charcoal, in others the legs were spotted with purple blood. Then the disease would rise to the hips, shoulders, arms and neck. And all had their mouths so infected that the gums rotted down to the roots of the teeth, nearly all of which fell out.

The disease spread among the men of our three ships to such an extent that by February of the 110 men in our expedition, not ten were in good health, and there was no one to aid the sick. Our captain, seeing our pitiable condition, and how widespread the disease had become, gave orders for prayers and orisons and an image of the Virgin Mary to be set up against a tree a bowshot from our fort. And he ordered Mass to be said there on the Sunday following, and all who could walk, both sick and well, to form a procession chanting the seven psalms of David and the Litany, praying the Virgin to be good enough to ask her dear Son to have pity on us.

And when the Mass had been pronounced and chanted before the image, the captain made a vow to go on pilgrimage to Our Lady of Rocquemando, if God would grant him grace to return safely to France. That day Philippe Rougemont of Amboise passed away, aged about 20 years.

the Indian cure

Cartier ordered an autopsy, and "the heart was found all white and shrunken, surrounded by a potful of water like date juice, the liver good, but the lungs all blackened and corrupted."

Twenty-five of them died, but the Indians had a cure, and passed it along: evergreen twigs, chopped, boiled in water, the liquid drunk, and the residue used as a poultice on leg sores. Using it, they

Roberval
The King's Protestant

In part it must have been the king's "holy war" with the Pope that led him to name Jean-François de la Rocque de Roberval—*a Protestant*—the chief, leader and captain of the would-be colony of New France. Three months before, Cartier had been granted the same commission, and through the spring of 1541, both men recruited a rag-tag coterie of emigrés (mostly reprieved convicts) for settlement in Canada. Cartier got there first, and by the time Roberval arrived in June, Cartier was on his way back to France with barrels of fool's gold and a few tall tales. Roberval's attempt at establishing a colony failed—the winter, disease, and the already-suspicious Iroquois saw to that. Roberval returned to France in 1543 to face lawsuits and financial ruin, and was murdered in 1562.

recovered so rapidly that they thought the Virgin had granted the requested miracle.

"And some of the sailors who had been suffering five or six years from the great pox were by this medicine completely cured . . . in eight days . . . a whole tree . . . was used up."

The magic was vitamin C, in which some evergreens are very rich. (It is now thought that the tree used was white cedar.)

twenty-four strings of wampum

When ready to sail in the spring, Cartier tricked Donnacona and four other men into visiting his fort, then seized them and drove off the other Indians. Next day the people tried to ransom the chief with twenty-four strings of wampum—probably the band's total stock of ready cash. But Cartier promised to bring him back in a year's time. The men and the children were taken to France, where they soon died of smallpox or some other European plague.

On Cartier's return *five* years later, he tried to convince the Indians that only the chief had died, the others remaining in France "as great lords." But the Indians treated this lie with the contempt it deserved, and refused to have anything to do with him. His third voyage was a dismal failure. The Iroquois, on whom he had depended for his earlier success, had become confirmed enemies.

Meanwhile the King had appointed a governor, one Jean-François de la Rocque de Roberval, who sailed separately a year after Cartier. They met at St. John's, Newfoundland, Roberval heading for the Kingdom of the Saguenay, and Cartier heading for France with a cargo of fool's gold, and for eventual disillusionment and embittered retirement.

Montreal in 1535

The first popular account of Cartier's voyages to Canada was published not in France or England, but in Italy in 1556, by Giovanni Battista Rasmusio. Strange? Not really, considering that spies of all nations loitered around port-city docks, picking up bits of new information from returning crews. Also, it seems that as soon as an explorer had made his report to his king and company, propagandists swiftly let the word out on new discoveries and claims, thereby hoping to frustrate rivals at home and abroad. It is hard to say exactly how Rasmusio came into possession of Cartier's notebooks. (There is some evidence that Cartier himself published these in 1545, but no copies have survived.) In any case, much of what is known about Cartier's Canada, including this view of Hochelaga, is a Venetian's impression of a Frenchman's account.

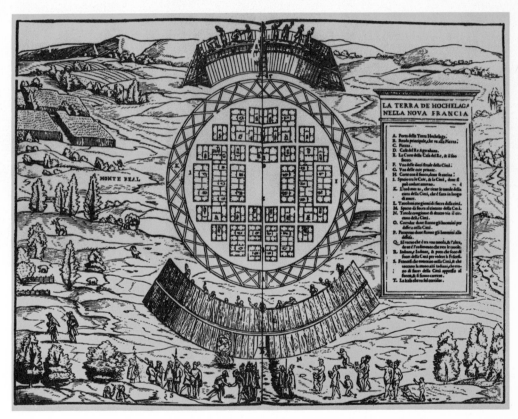

Rasmusio's sketch of Hochelaga, based only on verbal descriptions, looks more like a medieval fortress than an Indian palisade. The floor plan of the fort shows Chief Agouhana's lodge and surrounding buildings at the centre, cultivated fields and a hill called Monte Real outside the gates. The scene at the very bottom shows Cartier greeting the village's emissaries.

The Explorer's Life

Who were these men who named themselves explorers, and coaxed kings, queens and the wealthy families of Europe to put up the money and ships for their escapades? Some, like Henry Hudson and Thomas James, were sailors and navigators – men trained to know ships, maps, instruments and the unpredictable sea. Others, like Martin Frobisher and Jacques Cartier, were privateers and pirates – soldiers of fortune quick with pistol and cutlass. Still others, the likes of Humphrey Gilbert, Francis Drake, and Walter Raleigh, were the crazy young men of the Court of Queen Elizabeth – swashbuckling daredevils out for fame or fortune.

Martin Frobisher: pirate and privateer – shot by a Spaniard.

Humphrey Gilbert: one of Elizabeth's courtiers, would-be colonizer – lost at sea.

Henry Hudson: navigator, explorer for Holland, then England — set adrift with his son and six others in the Arctic by his crew.

While attempts to establish colonies elsewhere in New France and New England were frustrated by wars with and among the Indians, the settlements of Acadia suffered little from such conflicts. However, when competition for the fur trade monopoly of the region came to a head, settlers lived in constant terror of the axe, the musket and the noose. Above, an arrogant Menou d'Aulnay orders the execution of his rival Charles de La Tour's colonists in 1645.

CHAPTER THREE

L'Acadie

We fitted out two barks which were loaded with the timbers from the houses of Ste.-Croix, to transport them to Port Royal, 25 leagues off, which had been judged a much milder and more temperate place to live.

Champlain, *Les Voyages de la Nouvelle France*, 1632

As a young lawyer in France, Marc Lescarbot lost a case that he clearly should have won, and was so embittered by the miscarriage of justice that he decided to throw up his profession and go to Acadia as a colonist. A client of his, Jean de Biencourt de Poutrincourt, had just agreed to join his friend Pierre du Gua de Monts in the founding of a colony in what is now Nova Scotia. In 1603, de Monts had received from the King a ten-year monopoly on the fur trade.

This was not the first attempt by the French to found an Acadian colony. As early as 1598, they had made a plantation on Sable Island, a narrow spit of land lying on the edge of the fishing banks a hundred miles southeast of Canso. A crazy place to found a colony, perhaps, but not so crazy as Frobisher Bay on Baffin Island, which had been the choice of the English twenty years earlier.

The founder, the Marquis de la Roche-Mesgouez, intended to people his colony with convicts, to whom he offered to sell their freedom for substantial sums. When this racket was forbidden by the courts, la Roche persuaded the *parlement* of Rouen to hand over to him 250 "vagabonds and beggars." Out of these he chose forty, and sent them to Sable Island with pigs and cattle. But their main activities seem to have been sealing and whaling. For a year or two cargoes of oils and skins were shipped to France. Then, in 1602, no supplies were sent out. In 1603, the supply ship arrived to find that the colony's leaders had been murdered and only eleven colonists remained.

The colonizing effort by de Monts in 1604 was a much sounder affair. Its chronicler, Lescarbot, was a fluent writer in French and Latin. He spent a year at Port Royal, the first permanent settlement in Acadia, and described its life in detail. He was not only an educated observer, but a man who liked to grow his own vegetables, hunt his own meat and travel with parties of Indians. He often wrote from first-hand knowledge.

The voyage of 1604 got off to an early start and made a good passage: "On May 6 they reached land at a certain harbour in 44° latitude, where they found a Captain Rossignol of Havre de Grace trading in furs with the natives contrary to the King's prohibition. Consequently, they seized his ship and called the harbour Port Rossignol, so in his misfortune he had the consolation that a good, safe harbour on that coast bears his name." It was later renamed Liverpool by the English.

At Port Mouton they built tilts, like those of the

The first history of New France was compiled and written by Marc Lescarbot, a young lawyer, poet and naturalist who lived in Port Royal in 1606. His talent for music and theatre prompted him to write and produce the first play staged in North America, Théâtre de Neptune. *A bachelor until 50, he also wrote a tract on polygamy.*

The first colonists were an odd lot: reprieved prisoners, farmers and a few tradesmen. They dressed in baggy, homespun coats and breeches, and, to the Indians' amazement, all wore hats.

savages, while waiting for news of the other ship, which carried the provisions and other necessities for the support and maintenance of those who were to winter in the country, numbering about a hundred people."

De Monts next explored the estuary of the Annapolis River where Port Royal would later be built, made a circuit of the Bay of Fundy, and explored the St. John River upstream for hundreds of miles, finding wild vines, wild onions, and "many other good herbs." By good luck the French had lit upon two of the finest agricultural areas in the Atlantic region—the Annapolis Valley and the Valley of the St. John. Guided by Indians, they also found the route from the St. John to the St. Lawrence, thus linking Acadia with Cartier's Canada.

Poutrincourt was the first to recognize the great possibilities of Port Royal and the Annapolis Valley. As soon as he laid eyes on it, he asked that it be ceded to him in seigneury—which was promptly done. He thus became the first great landlord in Acadia, and principal advocate of a strong colony there. He was to spend years trying to promote the colony and bankrupted himself in its service. He failed in the end only because he could not raise the money to continue.

voluntary submission

That first winter, after sending Poutrincourt home with a cargo of furs, de Monts and most of the party, including Samuel Champlain, spent on an island off the coast of what is now Maine, and "the savages from all the surrounding country came freely among us . . . in certain matters they even made M. de Monts a judge between them, which is the beginning of voluntary submission, whence one may entertain the hope that they will soon adopt our way of life."

The island was a poor choice: "When wood or water were needed the river had to be crossed . . . both painful and tedious, so you often had to reserve the boat a day in advance to get the use of it. On top of this came cold and snow and frost so hard that wine froze in the casks, and had to be shared out by weight . . . . Soon unknown diseases broke out, like those already described by Captain Jacques Cartier." Lescarbot then goes on to describe terminal cases of scurvy. "Thirty-six died of this sickness, and thirty-six to forty more were laid low, but recovered with the coming of spring."

scurvy everywhere

They knew that Cartier had been shown a cure by the Indians, but they didn't know what it was. After a relief party of forty men arrived in early summer, they tore down the buildings and moved them piecemeal across the Bay of Fundy to Port Royal. Because they thought scurvy might by contagious, they burned the dead men's bedding.

At Port Royal they planted gardens, raised cattle and pigs, and built a substantial fort with two-storied dwelling houses and covered walks for winter. Lescarbot took great pleasure in working the ground:

I can say truthfully that I never did so much manual work . . . digging and cultivating my gardens, fencing them against the greed of the hogs, making terraces, laying out straight walks, building outhouses, sowing wheat, rye, barley, oats, beans, peas, herbs, watering them, so great was my desire to have personal experience of the soil . . . . The summer days were too short for me, and in spring I often worked by moonlight.

In the last months of the colony's second winter, supplies again ran low, and twelve more men died of scurvy. Half the colonists, the Roman Catholic priest and the Protestant minister among them, had now died for lack of any trace of vita-

The First Settlements

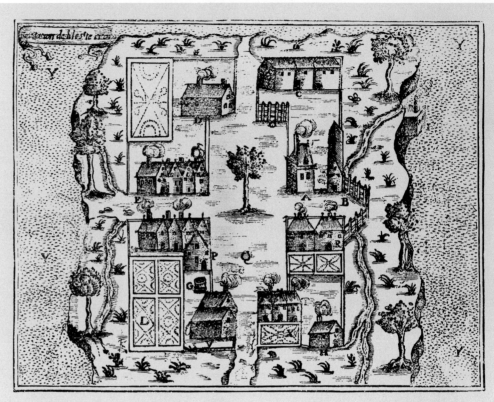

A Logis du fieur de Mons.
B Maifon publique ou l'on paffoit le temps durant la pluie.
C Le magafin.
D Logement des fuiffes.
E La forge.
F Logement des charpentiers
G Le puis.
H Le four ou l'on faifoit le pain.

I La cuifine.
L Iardinages.
M Autres Iardins.
N La place où au milieu y a vn arbre.
O Paliffade.
P Logis des fieurs d'Oruille, Champlain & Chandore.
Q Logis du fieur Bouley, & autres artifans.

R Logis ou logeoièt les fieurs de Geneftou, Sourin & autres artifans.
T Logis des fieurs de Beaumont, la Motte Bourioli & Fougeray.
V Logement de noftre curé.
X Autres iardinages.
Y La riuiere qui entoure l'ifle.

The settlement on Ile Ste-Croix off New Brunswick's south coast was home for the first French colonists from 1604-1605. This sketch based on Champlain's diary shows (A) De Monts' house (B) the public house (C-M) the magazine, lodgings, forge, well, bake-ovens, kitchen and gardens (P-T) lodgings for Champlain, other officials and craftsmen, and (V) the priest's house.

min C in their diet. Poutrincourt tried to get a priest to go out on the next voyage, but "there was no means of dragging one of them out of Paris," says Lescarbot. Though a devout Catholic himself, he ran the New World's first Sunday School for the illiterate members of the colony, using John Calvin's translation of the Bible.

drinking with pirates

De Monts and most of the other survivors of the first winter went back to France in September. Next May, Poutrincourt took a ship out again with Lescarbot in attendance, making notes. Near the Azores they fell in with another ship. "We asked where they came from. They replied that they were Newfoundlanders, and offered us their company, which we refused with thanks. They then drank our health and we theirs, and they went off in another direction, but after inspecting their ship, which was coated with weeds, we concluded that they were pirates, and had been at sea a long time looking for a prize."

The voyage was long and troubled, but Lescarbot was too busy with his journal to be bored:

Storms were often preceded by dolphins, which surrounded our ship by thousands and played about very pleasantly. Some of them came to grief by approaching too close to us, for we had a watchman below the bowsprit, . . . harpoon in hand, who transfixed them more than once and hauled them on board with the help of other crewmen who drew them up with iron hooks (called gaffs) attached to the end of a long pole.

. . . When he was cut open we bathed our hands in the warm blood, which is supposed to strengthen the sinews . . . . The meat tastes just like pork, and his bones are arranged not like those of a fish, but of a quadruped . . . . We saw other large fish far off displaying more than half an acre of their backs above

water and throwing great fountains into the air to a height of more than two lances above the blow-holes in their heads . . . .

Sometimes, too, we had troublesome calms when we went swimming in the sea, danced on deck, and climbed to the cross-trees singing in concert. But when a small cloud appeared on the horizon we abandoned our sports to prepare for a squall . . . which could have upset our ship if the men were not ready to carry out the captain's orders.

Ships still navigated "by guess and by God." Near the edge of the Banks of Newfoundland they met another French ship and compared estimates of position. There was a difference of 180 miles. On June 18, they ran into the Gulf Stream (still uncharted) and "for the space of three days the sea water was very warm and our wine in the hold also, though the air was no warmer than before." Then they met the Labrador Current, and "we thought we were in the month of January." Off southern Newfoundland on June 23, they furled their sails to spend the day fishing and catching seabirds on baited hooks. In this way they killed thirty fulmars, birds as big as ducks. "We also caught some dog fish, whose skins our carpenters preserved, to be used for sanding wood for furniture."

a worthless monopoly

At Canso they learned that the Basques had again ignored the King's grant of the fur trade to de Monts, and had made off with the entire beaver catch from Cape Breton, amounting to six thousand pelts. It was becoming obvious that de Monts's monopoly was worthless, and that financial ruin was likely.

They did not reach Port Royal until July 27, two months and fourteen days from France, at a time when fishing ships made the voyage in three

By all accounts everyone ate well at Port Royal: stone-ground whole wheat bread baked in the brick oven (above), sturgeon, lobster, crabmeat, mussels, vegetables including corn, squash, beans and cabbages. "Of all their meats none is so tender as moose-meat . . . and none so delicate as beaver's tail," wrote Lescarbot. A bottle of wine topped off the menu.

Opposite page: *With few exceptions, the European attempts to establish permanent colonies were met with caution and hostility. When trade agreements and alliances broke down, bows and arrows were no match for French- and English-made firearms.*

40

Etablissement des Francois dans le Canada.

Ce Païs fut découvert en 1504 par des pecheurs Basques, Normands, et Bretons,
ensuite en 1508 par Thomas Aubert de Dieppe qui amena en France des Sauvages du Païs,
ensuite par Jean Verrazan qui en 1523 y fut envoié par François 1. mais en 1534 Jacques
Cartier Capitaine Malouin prit possession de ces Païs au nom du Roi, depuis ce tems les
Français avoient essaié plusieurs fois d'établir une bonne Colonie le long du Fleuve de St. Laurent
mais les obstacles qu'ils y avoient rencontrés ne leur permit pas de la rendre solide avant
l'année 1608 où monsieur de Champlain aiant achevé la découverte de ces Païs, fonda la
Ville de Quebec Capitale du Canada ou nouvelle France, il fit alliance avec les Algonkins et autres nations Sauvages, et fut obligé d'aller a la guerre avec eux Contre
les Iroquois qu'ils vainquirent par le secours des Français et de leurs armes a feu,
ce qui les rendit respectables a toutes
ces nations

41

Though most early drawings done in Canada are crude in style, illustrations, like this one *(probably made by the Jesuit missionary Louis Nicholas between 1667 and 1675, and one of dozens in the* Codex Canadensis*)* show something of the white man's fascination for the Indian's ways. Two tattooed men are using barbed spears and nets to catch shallow-water fish.

to four weeks. By the time they reached Port Royal, the colonists had abandoned it. Believing that no supply ship was coming, they had set out in longboats to join the fishing fleet, leaving only two watchmen to guard the colony. Fortunately, a party guided by Indians managed to find the missing colonists and bring them back.

the Promised Land

They began planting gardens on July 28 – late, but apparently successful. Fortunately they had no frost until December. That year they planted radishes, turnips, cabbages, wheat, rye, flax and hemp (the latter probably grown mainly for fibre). Lescarbot was entranced by the Annapolis Valley: "We found almost continuous grasslands for a distance of twelve leagues, among which flow numerous brooks rising in the nearby hills and mountains." He compared it with the Promised Land of the Hebrews.

In summer and autumn the colonists feasted on shellfish and game, including Canada geese and migrating snow geese. They had so much wine that everyone was allowed a pint a day. Good wine every day in winter would be "a sovereiign remedy against scurvy," Lescarbot believed – a good guess. High-quality wine may have quite a bit of ascorbic acid – oxydized wine has none. Friendly Indians supplemented their game supply, and traded the products of their own agriculture: corn, beans, pumpkins, tobacco. No one in North America ever enjoyed better relations with the neighbouring Indians than the Acadian French. Nevertheless, two of the colonists were killed by a hostile tribe when they ventured too far south along the New England coast.

Poutrincourt, the seigneur of Port Royal, established that winter among the men of his own class (the fifteen gentlemen) a club that Lescarbot described in detail:

I shall relate how in order to keep our table cheerful and well-provisioned, an Order was established in the dining hall of M. de Poutrincourt, which was named The Order of Good Cheer, first suggested by Champlain. In this Order each man of the said table was appointed chief steward in his turn, which was once every two weeks. Now this person was required to see that we were well and honourably provided . . . there was no one who, two days before his turn arrived, failed to go hunting or fishing, and to return with some delicacy in addition to our ordinary fare . . . the ruler of the feast, having first overseen the cuisine, came marching in, napkin on shoulder, rod of office in hand, and around his neck the collar of the Order, which was worth more than four crowns; after him all the members of the Order, each carrying a dish . . . .

And at night, before giving thanks to God, he handed over the collar of the Order to his successor, with a cup of wine, and they drank to each other . . . . We . . . had plenty of game such as ducks, grouse, grey and white geese, partridge, plover and other birds; besides moose, caribou, beaver, otter, bear, rabbits, wild cats, raccoons and other animals caught by the Indians, of which we made dishes well worthy of the cook shop in the Rue aux Ours and even better, for none of our meats is so tender as moose (of which we also made excellent pies) or so delicate as beaver tail . . . .

At these ceremonies we always had twenty or thirty Indians, men, women, girls and children, who observed our style of service. Free bread was given them, as one would do to the poor. But as for Sagamos Membertou and other chiefs who visited occasionally, they sat at table, eating and drinking like us.

All the Indians of Acadia were either Micmacs or Malecites – both of Algonkian stock, though some writers have recently brought forward evidence to suggest that the Malecite were a tribe of half-breeds descended from Indians who had worked for European fishermen, interbred with them, adopted some of their customs, and incorporated elements of their language. Lescarbot gives support to this theory with the statement that some of the Indians spoke a language that was "half Basque."

Those who shared the feasts at Port Royal were certainly Micmacs, belonging to what some ethnologists call "the Algonkian birchbark culture." The Micmacs did, indeed, put birchbark to a surprising variety of uses, sewing it into waterproof covering for canoes, stretching it over poles to make tents, even folding and stitching the stuff into cooking pots. But the Micmacs did not depend upon birchbark to the extent of their northern neighbours. They wove excellent baskets and made pottery, though they quit making it as soon as metal pots arrived from France. They also developed very quickly a taste for French bread and began trading meat for it.

They were mainly a hunting people, but, perhaps because they lived in one of the most fertile parts of Canada, they had adopted agriculture. They bartered a few vegetables with the French – mainly corn, beans and pumpkins – but did not raise the vast crops of corn, beans, squash and melons that were the mainstay of the Iroquois and the Hurons.

roots

The political organization of the Acadian tribes was so loose and anarchic that the French steadfastly refused to believe it, investing the chiefs with an authority that they never possessed. A chief among the Micmacs was a man of high prestige and honour, a leader in the hunt and in the tribal council, but certainly not a head of state, issuing orders to his inferiors – the only kind of political organization that the French at that period could even imagine.

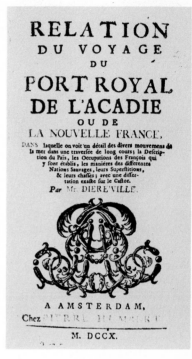

**RELATION
DU VOYAGE
DU
PORT ROYAL
DE L'ACADIE
OU DE
LA NOUVELLE FRANCE.**
DANS laquelle on voit un détail des divers mouvemens de la mer dans une traversée de long cours; la Déscription du Païs, les Occupations des François qui y sont établis, les manieres des differentes Nations Sauvages, leurs Superstitions, & leurs chasses; avec une dissertation exacte sur le Castor.
Par Mr. DIERE'VILLE.

A AMSTERDAM,
Chez PIERRE HUMBERT

M. DCCX.

Pierre Dièreville's account of his voyage to Port Royal is a curious compendium. As diary, it notes that a cabin boy was whipped en route "to calm the winds." As a naturalist's journal (the author was a "doctor"), it records the flora and fauna of Acadia. And as a "cookbook," it is the first important work on North American food and its preparation.

**Françoise-Marie La Tour
Actress in a Tragedy**

When Françoise-Marie Jacquelin married Charles de La Tour at Port Royal in 1640, she was 38, possibly a former Paris actress. Her husband, who had come to Acadia at 14 (and fathered three Métis children), had inherited the French claim from Charles de Biencourt in 1623. His tiny settlement withstood repeated attacks by New Englanders. In 1636, however, his land and trade monopoly was challenged from within by Charles d'Aulnay. Twice Mme. La Tour ran d'Aulnay's blockade of the St. John River fort, reached France, and pleaded for supplies and the King's support. While her husband was in Boston mustering support from the English, d'Aulnay attacked and on Easter Sunday 1645, forced Mme. La Tour to surrender. One of the defendents was singled out to execute the others, while Mme. La Tour sat and watched, a rope around her neck. She died three weeks later.

The colonists often went hunting with the Indians, and one young man lived with them for six weeks in mid-winter, "without salt, bread or wine, sleeping on the ground on skins." To their amazement he returned at least as healthy as the men who had remained in the settlement, and healthier than some, for despite the abundance of wine and meat, seven more men died of scurvy that winter. They were all of the lower class—labourers, not members of the Order of Good Cheer.

Next year the colony planted large gardens, devised a means of boiling spruce gum into pitch to cover boat seams, and much to the astonishment of the Indians built a water-powered mill to grind flour. Unlike gunpowder, which seemed a kind of magic, the mill was something the Indians could fully understand, and they marvelled at its cleverness.

The colony flourished, but the company went bankrupt. Its failure was blamed on the Dutch, who, "led by a French traitor named La Jeunesse", captured almost the whole of the fur trade. De Monts' monopoly was revoked, no new colonists came out, and those already there fell into a state of despondency.

Poutrincourt declared that Port Royal would not be abandoned, even if he and his family had to live there alone with the Indians. Eight men volunteered to stay, on condition that he pay them wages that he could not afford. Reluctantly, he returned to France, promising to return next year with permanent settlers, including women and children. Port Royal, after three years, lay empty.

Lescarbot went back to France in 1607, received redress for the wrong he had suffered in court, and resumed his law practice. In 1609, he published the first *History of New France*, and continued bringing out new editions until 1618.

Poutrincourt did not return until 1610. The Indians, he found, had kept his settlement in perfect condition. Moreover, now that he had brought a priest, the principal men of the Micmac tribe came in readily to be changed into Frenchmen. (Under the law of the time a baptized Indian became a French citizen.) The great French missionary effort had begun.

Once again, Port Royal was occupied for three years, the colony being in charge of Poutrincourt's son, Charles de Biencourt. It was then attacked and destroyed by a Virginian privateer, Samuel Argall. He arrived when the French settlers were out on their farms, and some of them hunting with the Indians. There was no resistance. He demolished the *habitation*, hoisted the Cross of St. George over the ruins, and sailed away. The survivors spent the winter with the Indians, and next year began rebuilding Port Royal. After that, Acadia was never entirely abandoned by the French, and the government of France, from time to time, assisted in colonizing efforts. A peasant farming culture gradually took root in the Annapolis Valley and northward around the Minas Basin. These people became the *Acadiens* whom the English found there a century later.

There were many attempts by New Englanders to take Acadia, both by force and by infiltration (altogether, Port Royal was attacked nine times), but these efforts remained generally unsuccessful: not because of the strength of the French, whose numbers were pitiably small, but because the Indians were firmly on the French side, and hostile to the English.

Though Port Royal was sacked repeatedly, it was not finally captured by the English until 1710, when its garrison of 258 men was besieged by an army of 1,900. Though this was the only point held by the English in Acadia, it was the French capital, and consequently they claimed the entire region in the peace settlement. They renamed it Annapolis Royal (for their Queen Anne), fortified and garrisoned it, and made it into a flourishing port in their new colony of Nova Scotia.

Samuel Argall's sacking of Port Royal in 1613 (above) foreshadowed a century of strife between the French and the New Englanders over Acadia. In 1657, after years of in-fighting for control of the fur trade, the weakened colony was once again overrun by the English. The final defeat was to come a century later.

...and in the hour of our death

As the Church gained a better foothold in New France, religion became more of a part of the everyday ritual in most communities. In fact, many of the letters sent back to France by the early parish priests deplore the slight regard most colonists had for the Church, its commandments and rituals. All that changed with the coming of the Jesuits and Recollets. Artists, too, adopted Catholic themes – from the altar paintings of the Holy Family, to the votive panels commemorating local miracles. The best *ex-votos* were painted by people with little training, but their documentary honesty tells a great deal about the common tragedies of life.

This votive panel depicts a 2:00 A.M. canoe accident at Lévis in which two young women were drowned. Hung in the church vestibule, it reminded generations to follow that divine intervention (or quick thinking) had saved the lives of the two men and the third woman.

Ex-voto de Madame Riverin et ses quatre enfants *(1703) was painted to commemorate another near-disaster on the St. Lawrence. The four survivors—the wife and children of an obviously well-to-do member of the Quebec council—offer thanks to their patron saint, Anne.*

Well before John Guy established the first settlement at Cupids in 1610, English fishing "stores" and "flakes" were a unique feature of Newfoundland's harbours. In 1690, when the Dutch painter Gérard Edema toured the coast, he found the buildings more substantial but the cod-drying process (foreground) the same.

The Pirates of Harbour Grace

Sweet Creatures, did you truely understand
The pleasant life you'd live in Newfound-land,
You would with teares desire to be brought thither;
I wish you when you go faire wind, faire weather.

Robert Hayman, *Quodlibets*, 1628

Sheila O'Connor, commonly known as Sheila Na-gaira (which is Old Gaelic for "Sheila the Beautiful") had no thought of Newfoundland in her mind when she set out from her home in County Connacht, Ireland, in the spring of 1602 to join her aunt who was abbess of a French convent.

Sheila sailed on a small Irish ship, but was no more than a few days at sea when a Dutch raider seized the unarmed vessel and made prisoners of passengers and crew. The Dutch, at the time, were vassals of Spain, with which the English were carrying on a guerrilla warfare at sea. On England's side such bold privateers as the Drakes, Raleighs and Gilberts, skilled in the art of hit-and-run battles, were gradually bringing Spanish seapower to its knees.

One of these, Captain Peter Easton, in command of a squadron of three ships going to Newfoundland as convoy for the English fishing fleet, met and seized the Dutch raider, then continued his voyage with the liberated passengers and Dutch prisoners on board.

So Sheila became, by accident, the first Irish girl known to have settled in Canada. During the voyage she got to know one of Easton's lieutenants, a young man named Gilbert Pike. They were married (presumably by the captain under the rules of the sea), and before the end of the fishing season had taken fishing rooms at the small harbour of Mosquito, which lies between the fishing ports of Harbour Grace and Carbonear in Conception Bay.

Though the Pikes are thought to be the first married couple to have settled after the time of the Norse, all the main harbours of eastern Newfoundland were occupied and developed long before their arrival. Hundreds of English ships with thousands of fishermen were on the coast every year from May to September, and winter crews were left to build and repair the fishing rooms. There was a winter boatbuilding industry, and even a little farming; within seven years of the arrival of the Pikes, the first grist mill was built a few miles from their home.

Richard Whitbourne, a contemporary of the Pikes who wrote a book about Newfoundland addressed to King James, made much of early attempts at farming. His book, promoted by the king, became a national best-seller in England and did much to promote colonization. Within ten years of its publication in 1620, the Newfoundland colonies were larger than those of New France.

Besides the English, the Portuguese, the French, and (when not at war with England) the

George Calvert, otherwise known as Lord Baltimore (promoter of the American colony at Chesapeake Bay), made several attempts to establish a Newfoundland colony. An absentee landlord except for a brief stay in 1628, his claims were an easy mark for pirates such as Peter Easton and David Kirke.

No place in the world can claim as colourful a heritage of place names as Newfoundland – some derived from the days the first sailors, pirates and fishermen reached the island.

Spanish shared the Newfoundland fishery, but except for the English they fished exclusively from ships and took the fish home in saltbulk, undried. Because they had to buy salt in foreign markets, the English had developed the shore cure – sun-dried fish using little salt, requiring substantial shore installations for its manufacture. This explains why the English built "fishing rooms" all along the coast while other nationalities did not. Long before the end of the sixteenth century, they had created the Newfoundland outport with its stores and drying flakes very much as it still exists today. They had also established the markets – Italy, Spain, Portugal, and Brazil – that endured for the next three hundred and fifty years.

Fishing occupied only a few weeks each summer, ending in a frantic race to get the fish sun-cured in time to be shipped with the fleets leaving in autumn. Since fish could "sunburn" and spoil, drying had to be done only in sunny but cool weather. Fish had to be taken up or covered when rain threatened or the sun was too hot, then spread again. It involved a lot of work, but it produced a premium product that brought a far higher price than the saltbulk of the ship fishermen.

an abundance of food

Hunting and food-gathering were almost as important as fishing. Game was plentiful, and there was no competition from Indians, most of whom deserted the Avalon Peninsula as the fishermen arrived. Wild fruit was abundant, and the settlers soon discovered that some of the common species (those they named partridgeberries and bakeapples) could be preserved indefinitely without cooking or adding sugar merely by covering them with cold water. Stored thus in barrels, they remained fresh all winter. Spruce beer, also rich in vitamin C, was made at all seasons.

The chroniclers of the early Newfoundland colonies all reported with amazement that there was practically no sickness. At first they attributed this to the climate, but later discovered the connection with diet. Soon English ships were taking supplies of Newfoundland spruce beer as a remedy for scurvy, and continued using it until it was replaced by lime juice in the nineteenth century.

flourishing traders

Life in the New Land was neither easy nor desperately hard. Determined planters like Sheila and Gilbert Pike flourished, raised large families, and often reached a great age. Tradition credits her with living for a full century. Perhaps she did. If so, she lived to see the wilderness converted to a great mercantile colony, with some of the firms in the town of Carbonear, where she and her husband eventually settled, doing an international trade worth millions of pounds a year.

Whitbourne spent much of his working life in Newfoundland between 1579 and 1619. He saw Sir Humphrey Gilbert take possession of the country for Queen Elizabeth in 1583, saw the first official colonies founded, and rose himself from a common sailor to become the first Admiralty Court Judge appointed in Canada.

On his first voyage he sailed as a whaler with Master Cotton of Southampton, intending also to "trade with the savage people" and to make "trayne oil as the Biscaines [Basques] do there yearly in great abundance." They encountered no Indians on this voyage, but Whitbourne got to know them later, and gives one of the earliest first-hand accounts of the Newfoundland Beothuks:

They have great store of red ochre which they use to colour their bodies, bows and arrows and canoes withal, which canoes are built in shape like the wherries of the river of Thames, but that they are much longer, made with the rinds of birch trees which they

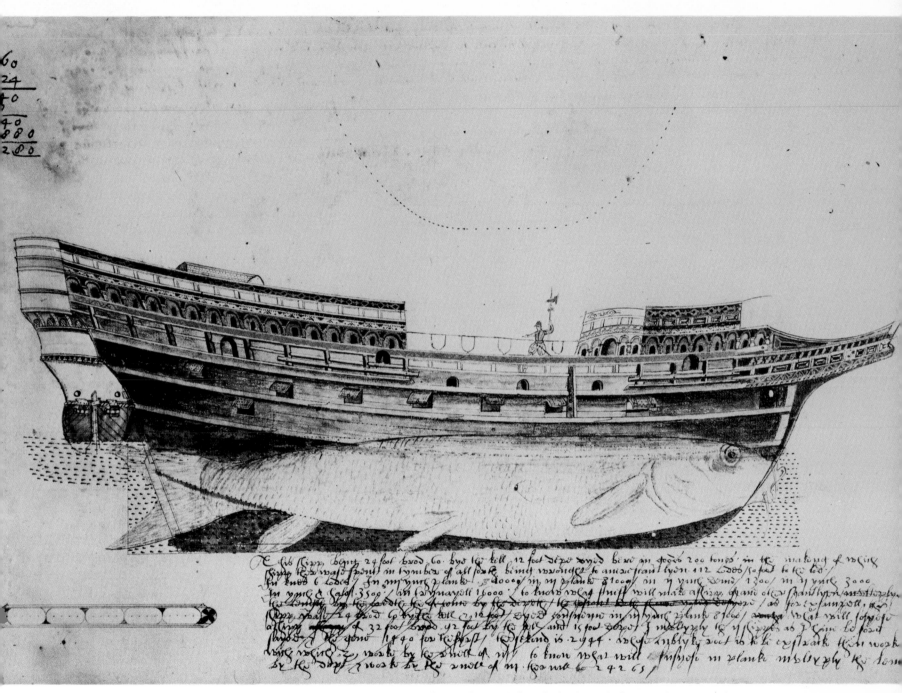

Designing and building vessels seaworthy enough to withstand the ocean's pounding and enemy's broadsides flourished as a trade through the three centuries of empire building. In this 1626 elevation of an English galleon, the shipwright has attempted to follow the belly-line of the fish in designing the hull.

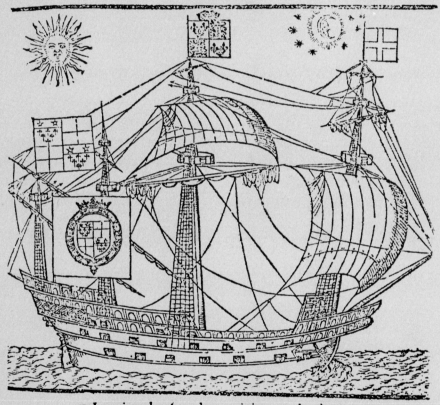

¶ A Regiment for the Sea: Conteynyng most profitable Rules, Mathematical experiences, and perfect knowledge of Nauigation, for all Coastes and Countreys: most needful and necessary for al seafaryng men and Trauellers, as Pilotes, Mariners, Marchaunts. &c. Exactly deuised and made, by William Bourne.

¶ Imprinted at London, nigh vnto the three Cranes in the Vintree, by Thomas Dawson, and Thomas Gardyner, for Iohn Wight.

To a great extent it was British naval power that gradually won the victory over Portugal, Spain, Holland and France. One of the handbooks for England's armada was William Bourne's A Regiment for the Sea *(1576) — a manual "most needful and necessary for all Seafaryng men."*

sow very artificially and close together and overlay every seam with turpentine.

He says the Beothuks kept wolves as domestic animals (but perhaps he meant husky dogs?), and "they mark their wolves in the ears as we do our sheep." Perhaps these are the same wolves that he mentions again: "It was well known to forty-eight persons of my company and divers other men that three several times the wolves and beasts of the country came down near them to the sea side where they were labouring about their fish, howling and making a noise, so that at each time my mastiff dog went unto them . . . the one began to fawn and play with the other, and so went together into the woods and continued with them, every of these times, nine or ten days, and did return unto us without any hurt."

The fish they were curing was cod, so abundant and valuable that they caught little else. One fish cargo that he lost to a pirate, Whitbourne valued at 850 pounds. Since a loaf of bread sold for a penny, and there were 240 pennies in a pound, we may reckon the value of this fish in present coinage at about $100,000.

thousands of fishers

The English fleet of the time, he reports, averaged two hundred and fifty ships a year. Portuguese, French, and Basque ships numbered about four hundred. Assuming the tonnage of the foreign ships to be about the same as the English, we arrive at the conclusion that more than ten thousand men must have been engaged in the Newfoundland fishery in those days. Nothing remotely comparable, either in numbers of men or in value of the product, was going on elsewhere in North America at the end of the sixteenth century. Even if Whitbourne's lost cargo was exceptional — and there's no reason to think it was — the annual value of the fishery in modern terms must have been around fifty million dollars.

From Admiralty to piracy

Piracy was a major occupation of the time when James I came to the English throne in 1603. When he withdrew Elizabeth's commissions to privateers and laid up the few ships owned by the Admiralty, many captains, including those who had sailed under Walter Raleigh, turned to piracy. The most successful of these was Peter Easton, who commanded as many as forty ships and made Newfoundland his base of operations. Richard Whitbourne was in his service all one summer:

In the year 1611, being in Newfoundland, at which time the famous arch-pirate Peter Easton came there, and had with him ten sail of good ships well furnished and very rich, I was kept eleven weeks under his command, and had from him many golden promises, and much wealth offered to be put into my hands, as it is well known. I did persuade him much to desist from his evil course; his entreaties to me then being that I would come for England to some friends of his, and solicit them to become humble petitioners to your Majestie for his pardon.

But having no warrant to touch such goods, I gave him thanks for his offer, only I requested him to release a ship that he had taken upon the coast of Guinea, belonging to one Captain Rashley of Foy in Cornwall, a man whom I knew but only by report, which he accordingly released. Whereupon I provided men, victuals and a freight for the said ship, and so sent her home to Dartmouth in Devon, though I never had so much as thanks for my kindness therein. And so leaving Easton I came for England and gave notice of his intention, letting pass my voyage that I intended for Naples, and lost both my labour and charges for before my arrival there was a pardon granted and sent him from Ireland.

After Harbour Grace, Easton fortified Ferryland, and from these bases made profitable raids against Spanish shipping, crowning his career by capturing the Spanish Plate Fleet off the Azores in 1614. Afterwards he served briefly with the Bey of Algiers, then retired to Villefranche, where he bought a palace, adopted the title of Marquis of Savoy, and later distinguished himself in a campaign by the Duke of Savoy against the Duchy of Mantua.

He and his associates co-operated with early colonists by taking their precious salt stores under protection, and seem to have avoided capturing English ships trading to Canada, though they had no compunction about looting English ships trading with the Spanish colonies. Perhaps the greatest damage they did was by enlisting fishermen and tradesmen into their crews. Sir William Vaughan, who founded a colony at Renewse in 1617, reported that more than fifteen hundred Newfoundlanders had sailed off in pirate ships "to the great hurt of the plantations."

Spanish treasure

Henry Mainwaring was Easton's rival and one of the great seamen of the time and author of the first English book on seamanship. He was an Oxford graduate, member of the Bar and master mariner at twenty-three, the year he was received at court and commissioned to go with an armed squadron in pursuit of Easton, then operating in the English Channel.

The government ships given to Mainwaring were unseaworthy, and he fitted out a second squadron at his own expense, giving Easton plenty of time to escape to Canada. So Mainwaring, foiled of his prey but wishing to recoup his investment, sailed off to capture Spanish treasure ships instead. After growing wealthy at Spain's expense, he crossed the Atlantic and occupied Easton's old

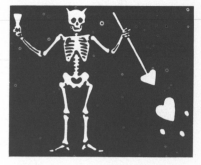

The skull-and-crossbones of the "Jolly Roger" (in one form or another) flew from the flagstaff of countless pirate vessels that plagued the coast of Newfoundland. (This version is the insignia of Edward Teach—"Bluebeard.") In 1614, Captain Henry Mainwaring was commissioned by England to catch another pirate, Peter Easton, who was terrorizing settlements and fleets. But to everyone's grief, Mainwaring himself turned pirate, snubbing the flags of his own and other nations for his private gain.

ENCOVRAGEMENTS,

For such as shall have intention to bee Vnder-takers in the new plantation of CAPE BRITON, now New Galloway in AMERICA,

BY MEE

LOCHINVAR,

Non nobis nati sumus; aliquid parentes, aliquid Patria, aliquid cognati postulant.

DREAD GOD

1625

EDINBVRGH,

Printed by Iohn Wreittoun. Anno Dom. 1625.

The Anglo-Scotch Company had tried to find settlers and backers for four years before they published this brochure of Encouragements for would-be settlers of New Galloway (Cape Breton).

fort at Harbour Grace. Easton, meanwhile, had moved to Ferryland.

The chronicler of the Cupids colony (founded by Bristol merchants in 1610) recorded Mainwaring's arrival with eight warships. When he sailed out of Harbour Grace on September 14, 1614, he took with him "four hundred mariners and fishermen, many volunteers, many compelled." But he denied in his memoirs that he had ever compelled a man in his life. Piracy was far more attractive than serving on the plantations.

From Newfoundland Mainwaring sailed to North Africa, and later to Villefranche, where he and Easton finally came face to face. There he received offers of command from three governments. The Bey of Tunis offered him permanent command of his fleet. Spain offered him a salary of twenty thousand gold ducats. England offered him a pardon and a knighthood. He accepted this and was made lieutenant of the port of Dover, was returned to parliament, and became Vice-Admiral and commander of the fleet. He carried on a vigorous campaign that for a time suppressed piracy in the North Atlantic. Under the commissions that he arranged in the 1620s, a number of important pirate vessels were brought into Newfoundland as prizes, among them the hundred-ton *Heart's Desire*. He ended his career fighting for Charles I against Cromwell.

terror of privateers

There were periods of peace when first England, then France, had enough seapower to police Canadian waters, but after the Treaty of Utrecht in 1713, chaos returned. While Quebec enjoyed its "long peace," the coasts were terrorized by an epidemic of piracy and privateering.

The most daring rogue of this period was a Newfoundlander named John Phillips, who had come from England as a shipwright, failed to get work in his trade at Placentia, and moved on to St. Peters (now called Saint-Pierre). There he formed a conspiracy with other malcontents and stole a ship owned by a New England trader. Only five out of a much larger band of conspirators had the nerve to go through with the plan, but those five soon augmented their numbers from the crews of captured ships.

Phillips became the terror of the Atlantic. In eight months, he ran down and captured at least thirty-three ships, some of them armed, and one that was actually fitted out for war, mounting twelve guns.

a gory end

His end was violent and gory. In April 1724, he took a fishing ship on the Banks, transferred his crew to it, and allowed some of the captured men to sail off in his old ship. Among those he forced to serve was Andrew Haraden, owner of the captured vessel, a new ship whose topsides were not quite finished. Within three days, Haraden had formed a conspiracy with the carpenter, Cheesman, and other impressed pirates to recapture the ship.

Pretending to work on the bulwarks, they moved all the axes, adzes, and hammers up on deck. Waiting for Haraden's signal, they suddenly overpowered the pirates. The mate, John Nutt, and the chief gunner, James Sparkes, were unceremoniously flung over the side. Phillips, hearing the uproar from his cabin, came rushing on deck, where Cheesman was waiting for him with a caulking hammer. The first blow smashed Phillips' jaw. Then Haraden finished him off with an axe. Ten of the pirates were brained and flung overboard, the others chained below under guard. Haraden then retook command of his ship and sailed her to Boston with Phillips' head hanging as a trophy from the yard-arm.

The bloodiest pair of predators in Canadian

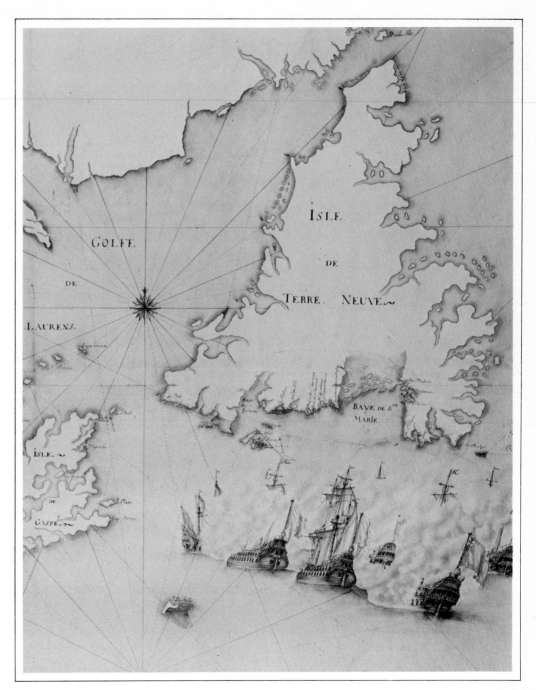

The dramatic cartouche of the fleet emerging from the fogs of Newfoundland takes up more space than the few fine-print place names in this detail from a 1696 map of Nouvelle France.

John Mason's Isle

There were less than sixty people living at Cuperts Cove (now Cupids) when John Mason arrived as governor in 1616. When he left ten years later—soon to found the colony of New Hampshire—he had seen tiny settlements crop up at Ferryland, Renewse and Bristol's Hope. A curious feature of Mason's map is the spelling of place names: some French, some English, and some (Ile of Diamonds, Petit Harbor) both. The legend is a French-English stab at Latin.

history were Edward Cobham and Maria Lindsay, who operated in the Gulf of St. Lawrence, preying on supply ships and capturing cargoes of furs. Because they sank every ship they captured and murdered everyone who fell into their hands, they went undetected for twenty years. Then this pair of escaped English criminals retired to France, bought an estate near Le Havre, and founded an aristocratic family. Cobham became a magistrate, but on his deathbed confessed his piracies and ordered the account published.

Many other famous pirates, including Bartholomew Roberts and Edward Bellamy, operated in Canada in the early eighteenth century. Bellamy had great influence among the "lower orders." He believed men of all classes could govern themselves by consensus, and introduced a form of democracy among his crews. The taste for self-determination that thousands of fishermen acquired from such leaders left them a permenently unruly class, impatient with authority. Some of them became "masterless men," living as outlaws hunted by English marines. Others took part in organized social revolt, which continued right down into the early twentieth century.

revered outlaws

Newfoundland's picturesque place names are also a pirate legacy: Happy Adventure, Heart's Desire, Bonaventure and Black Joke Cove are examples of the scores of places named for pirate ships. Kelly's Island, Turk's Gut and Tirk's Cove were named for the pirates themselves.

Though all were outlaws, they were not all villains. Bellamy, Easton and Mainwaring, among others, are remembered in folk tradition with great affection. In Newfoundland's Conception Bay, where Easton spent four years, many people today bear his surname, possibly from the old custom of adopting the name of a patron or leader.

A Whale Female and the Windlais whereby the Whales are brought on shore

The whale hunt was already an established annual practice for the Basques and Portuguese in 1587, when John Davis reached the Labrador coast. Whalers then "flensed" their catch alongside the ship. By 1650, when this drawing was made, the animals were towed by windlasses (marked E in the picture) onto shore, where the blubber was cut away with long-handled knives, and the valuable "train oil" was "tried out" or extracted.

57

The Cataract of NIAGARA, some make this Water Fall to be half a League while others reckon it no more than a hundred Fathom

A View of ye Industry of ye Beavers of Canada in making Dams to stop ye Course of a Rivulet, in order to form a great Lake, about wch they build their Habitations. To Effect this; they fell large Trees with their Teeth, in such a manner as to make them come Cross ye Rivulet, to lay ye foundation of ye Dam; they make Mortar, work up, and finish ye whole with great order and wonderfull Dexterity. The Beavers have two Doors to their Lodges, one to the Water and the other to the Land side. According to ye French Accounts.

To call this "View of ye Industry of ye Beavers of Canada" an exaggeration would be putting it mildly. Ridiculous as it now seems, the drawing was part of Herman Moll's "New and Exact Map of the Dominions . . ." and was probably based on the accounts of Louis Hennepin (see page 93). It shows an "assembly line" of beavers carrying stones on their tails and "armfuls" of timber to the construction site at their dam and lodge at the cataract of Niagara.

CHAPTER FIVE

The Beaver Hat

*. . . everywhere, too, we find the Iroquois,
who like an obtrusive phantom . . . prevent the
tribes from five or six hundred leagues
about us from coming down hither, laden with
furs that would make this country overflow
with immense riches. . . .*

Father Jérôme Lalemant, *Relation, 1659-60*

Throughout the European Middle Ages, furs were status symbols worn almost exclusively by men of the nobility, sometimes as badges of office – ermine for judges and kings, sable for great lords – and in some instances their use was regulated by law. Commoners might not wear them at all, nobles might wear only furs prescribed for their various ranks.

Most furs were rare and expensive. They came from Russia and Poland, and a few from Scandinavia and the forests of Germany, but all were funnelled through the monopoly of the Hanseatic League, a federation of German trading towns dating from the thirteenth century. The demand was small. The only fur in common use was beaver, made into felt for the hat trade. Hatters on the continent were using fur felt by 1465. Its first known use in England was in 1510, but by 1528 the word "beaver" was already a synonym for a hat, and beaver fur was also being used in London to make felt for boots.

Since beaver was in some demand, the fisher-men of the sixteenth century were mildly interested when they discovered the Indians would exchange pelts for cheap cloth and cheaper hardware. Beaver was the fur-bearing animal most hunted by the northern Indians, for its meat as well as its fur. Beaver robes – five to eight furs sewn together – were their choice for winter garments, and because it was plentiful, it was this fur that they most often traded. So the Basques, followed by the English and French, began taking trade goods on their whaling and fishing expeditions, and could dispose of the pelts they acquired at a good profit. But even as late as 1534, Cartier described North American fur as "a thing of small value."

However, forty years after his last voyage, the merchants of Cartier's home town were fitting out expeditions for furs alone, and a collection at Paris in 1583 was valued at twenty thousand crowns. By 1591, the French were trading needles, awls, knives, hatchets and cooking pots to the Indians of the St. Lawrence, and were making arrowheads and spearheads of iron especially for the Indian trade. The northern tribes promptly abandoned the use of stone weapons and tools for these more effective ones. So the Iron Age, among the Indians, arrived with the fur traders, and may well have been the reason the Montagnais-Micmac-Algonkin allies seem to have driven the Iroquoians out of the St. Lawrence Valley by the end of the

Samuel Champlain published the complete account of his early voyages in 1632, after he had returned to France from his imprisonment in England. The book contains the first map to show the interior of New France with any accuracy (of the Great Lakes only Michigan is missing), and includes the first extensive lexicon of the native languages.

sixteenth century.

During the following century, the popularity of the beaver hat increased rapidly, and the fur trade with it. One of the early Jesuit priests reported that up to twenty trading ships called annually at Tadoussac, the post at the mouth of the Saguenay River, taking twenty-two thousand beaver pelts in one year, and averaging twelve to fifteen thousand.

Lynx, fox, otter, marten and muskrat were added gradually as the market for these dressed furs rose with the rise of the middle class, and traders and businessmen began aping the fashions of the nobility.

native middlemen

New France was the only colony founded on the fur trade, but the English in Virginia and New England, the Dutch on the Hudson River, and later the English in Hudson Bay, all began trading in furs. Most of these came from the Canadian Shield, traded from tribe to tribe from places as distant as Hudson Bay and the Hudson River. And a great class of Indian middlemen arose among the Hurons and Iroquois, tribes that did little trapping themselves but travelled far and wide, trading their corn, beans, squash and tobacco for the pelts collected by the hunting tribes. The Hurons were the more successful because they were at peace with the tribes to the north of the St. Lawrence, the traditional enemies of the Iroquois.

Under the influence of the white traders, Indian rivalries eventually turned into wars of attrition, but as the seventeenth century opened, tribal warfare was still a kind of savage sport, conducted with small raids and elaborate ritual. The object was to win glory, take scalps, capture a few prisoners to be tortured, and, if they proved to be very brave, to be eaten, as a means of acquiring their virtue.

Even this kind of war, carried on for many years, could have longterm effects, and by the time Champlain set foot to earth in Canada in 1603, the Montagnais and Algonkins had displaced the Iroquoians of the St. Lawrence Valley. He found them celebrating a great raid in which a hundred enemy scalps had been taken:

As soon as we landed we went to the lodge of their head chief, named Anadabijou, where we found him and about eighty or a hundred of his companions making tabagie (which is to say feasting).

There were speeches and pipe smoking, and then:

. . . after they had made good cheer the Algonquins, one of the three nations, left their lodge and went apart by themselves in an open space. Here they drew up all their women and girls side by side, themselves behind, chanting in unison as I have already described. Then all the women and girls began to strip off their robes of skins, showing themselves completely naked, but keeping their ornaments, which are beads and interlaced ribbons made of porcupine quills dyed in many colors. After they had finished their chants they cried in unison, 'Ho! ho! ho!' At the same time the women and girls covered themselves with their robes which lay at their feet, and rested briefly, and then when the singing began they dropped their robes as before.

They do not move about as they dance but make gestures and motions of the body, lifting only one foot to stamp on the ground. While this dance was being performed the Algonquin chief, whose name was Besouat, sat before the women and girls between two poles on which hung the scalps of their enemies . . . They also pitted against one another two men of each nation, whom they made to run, and whichever was swiftest in the race won a prize.

The ritual must have come as a shock to Samuel Champlain, born a commoner and a Protes-

No authentic portrait of Champlain is known to exist, but we do know that he was thin and wiry, and of a height below average. Artists in the nineteenth century, however, pieced together fact and fiction, and most views of Champlain bear at least some resemblance to the one above from Picturesque Canada.

tant, his father a naval officer, his uncle a ship's captain. He had served in the French army during the reconquest of Brittany in 1598 at the end of the religious wars, then took service as a sailor with Spain.

compromise peace

He first came to Canada in 1603, as passenger on a fur-trading ship, then served as geographer to de Monts in Acadia, and when the Port Royal colony went bankrupt returned to the St. Lawrence as de Monts' deputy, armed with yet another fur-trading charter. He reached Tadoussac on June 3, 1608, to find Basque fur traders in armed conflict with de Monts' men. He patched up a compromise peace, then sailed upriver looking for a suitable place to plant his colony of twenty-eight.

On arrival I could find nothing better than the headland of Quebec, as it is called by the savages, which was covered with nut trees. Immediately I set some of our men to work cutting them down to make room for our settlement, others sawing planks, others digging the cellar and ditches, and others bringing up our freight from Tadoussac in the barque.

Soon Champlain found that members of the company were plotting to kill him and to turn Quebec over to the Basques. One conspirator turned informer, on promise of a pardon, and the others were promptly put under lock and key. Then there was a full-dress trial, after which the ringleader was hanged and his three lieutenants were sent back to France. The others were pardoned. By this combination of firmness and mercy, Champlain established an authority that was never afterwards questioned.

Champlain's Quebec consisted of three dwellings with a total of 1,500 square feet of floor: the upper stories surrounded by outside galleries, and a 650-square-foot storehouse with a full cellar – the

Although Champlain travelled mostly in canoes manned by Algonkin and Huron guides, he once proved his own paddling skill by shooting the treacherous Lachine Rapids (with some help).

L'habitation

Most high school students remember him as a dull name in history books, and tourists as a bridge in Montreal, but had it not been for Samuel Champlain, it is unlikely that France would have figured much in the Colonial Dream. He was a man of endless energy and many talents: sailor, farmer, fighter, artist (though not a good one), writer, architect, and the first town planner Canada had. At first he thought Port Royal in Nova Scotia was the best place to build a city, then Quebec, then Montreal. He probably saw Toronto Bay in 1615, but it was an unlikely place to start a settlement, and too far from France. He finally decided on Quebec and worked for 30 years to establish a town and society there. The drawing below is of the house he built in 1628.

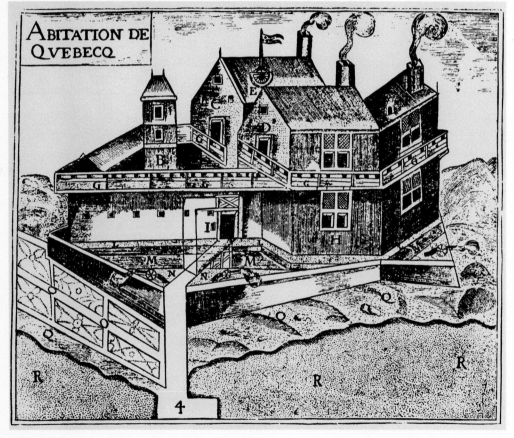

Champlain's house at Quebec was a three-storey "high-rise" apartment building surrounded by a wall and moat (M). His wife's and his own apartment were on the first floor (H). Workers' and artisans' lodgings were on the second and third levels, and the kitchen and forge were in the extension (F) on the right. (B) marks the pigeon coop, and (E) the "town clock" – a sundial.

entire settlement surrounded by a deep ditch and fortified with cannon. As winter advanced, most of his men fell sick with scurvy. The doctor and nine others died of it. Five more died of dysentery (food poisoning?). Only eight of the original twenty-eight survived the winter.

But reinforcements arrived next spring, and Champlain won the freedom of the backwoods by agreeing to join a Montagnais war party against the Mohawks. On this southern raid, he discovered Lake Champlain, fought his first skirmish, and returned with ten or twelve prisoners. On the way home the Indians stopped to torture one of the captives, "burning the poor wretch little by little to make him suffer the greatest torment . . . they tore out his nails and applied fire to the ends of his fingers and penis. Afterwards they scalped him and dripped a certain gum on his head, very hot . . . they begged me to take fire and do likewise . . . . " After an argument the Indians allowed Champlain to end the man's suffering with a musket-shot.

It is not surprising that Champlain, typical of his time, believed firmly that the devil acting through the Indians' shamans inspired the natives to commit these atrocities. But why the ritual torture of prisoners should have seemed more barbaric than the public burnings, brandings, guttings, and breakings-on-the-wheel so common in France at the time, we may well wonder.

The following summer – the third for the Quebec colony – Champlain and other Frenchmen helped the Algonkins storm an Iroquois fort on the Richelieu River. Eighty-five Iroquois were killed, fifteen others captured. Champlain managed to save the life of one of the prisoners by asking to have him for a slave. He escaped and spread the word that Champlain wanted an alliance with his people.

The wish was father to the thought, for the Iroquois were indeed anxious for peace. In spite of the image that the French managed to fasten upon them, they were a federation of peace-loving tribes, anxious to make alliances of mutual advantage with all their neighbours – as they did with many of them – but French relations with the northern tribes, and French encouragement of their raids into Iroquois territory, kept them in a constant state of defensive warfare.

the five nations

When New France was first settled, the Iroquois federation consisted of five tribes or nations living south of the St. Lawrence and the Great Lakes: from east to west they were the Mohawks, Oneidas, Onondagas, Cayugas and Senecas, all descended from the same stock as the Hurons, from whom they had separated some centuries earlier.

The federation was the work of the Onondaga chief, Hiawatha, a great political and religious leader of a stature comparable to Mohammed or Moses. He had conceived a scheme for a universal confederacy, each tribe maintaining its own council but electing members to a central government. More remarkable, the federation was to be permanently open to all who wished to join, its avowed aim being to abolish warfare altogether.

Failing to enlist the support of his own tribal council, Hiawatha went to the Mohawks and immediately converted the chief Deganawida, who became the political apostle of the new faith. Unlike Hiawatha, the Mohawk chief carried his tribal council with him, and dispatched two of his brothers to the neighboring Oneidas. That tribe took a year to debate the matter, then ratified the treaty that founded the federation.

The Onondagas, immediately to the west of the Oneidas, still refused to join, but the Cayugas, still further west, entered the union at the first opportunity, and combined with the other tribes to bring in the Onondagas by bribery and flattery. They were offered fourteen members on the governing council, in place of the ten assigned to the other three tribes, and their chief was given veto power over its decisions. On these terms they entered. In fact, however, their power was no greater than any other tribe, for all decisions of the council had to be unanimous, giving the veto, in effect, to everybody. The Onondagas, in turn, secured the accession of the powerful Senecas.

After the success of the federation, Hiawatha and Deganawida continued their efforts with missions to other tribes, even the distant Cherokees and Ojibwas. The Cherokee mission failed, but the Ojibwas formed an alliance with the federation that lasted for over a century, until it was finally ruptured, though not entirely broken, by the French.

five plus one more

Among their own people the federation was permanent and flexible. Not only were the conquered Hurons and Eries later welcomed into the five nations, but a sixth, the Tuscaroras, expelled from North Carolina by the whites, was accepted intact, given lands within the Iroquois domain, and seats on the council. Elements of other tribes defeated by white aggression also found refuge among them, until the "six nations" came to represent, in fact, the survivors of fourteen widely-scattered peoples from places as remote as the Dakotas, the Carolinas, Delaware and the Canadian Shield. The Iroquois name for the federation translated means "the great peace."

These, then, were the people whom the French confronted, and whose overtures for peace they consistently ignored or misunderstood.

In 1610, Etienne Brûlé, a youth of about eighteen who had already spent two winters at Quebec, went to live with the Indians in order to learn their languages. In exchange, Champlain, who was hop-

Louis Hébert
The Apothecary

Louis Hébert was working in his Paris drugstore when his wife's cousin first talked about moving to Canada. In the summer of 1606, he sailed with Champlain for Port Royal. Until the English destroyed the settlement in 1613, he was part-time "doctor"/part-time farmer at the fort, treating the illnesses of his company and the Indians. Hébert and Champlain met again in Paris in 1613, and four years later he sold his house, packed up his wife and three children, and headed for Quebec. With no horses or oxen, and no help from the Canada Company, he tilled the soil by hand, bringing in a sizeable harvest the following year. Bound by contract to keep up his medical practice, the farming was strictly "part-time" work. In 1626 at age 50, he suffered a fall on the river ice and never recovered.

ing to build a corps of interpreters, took a young Huron to France with him.

Brûlé became permanent French ambassador among the Hurons, but also travelled widely. He was the first European to reach what is now Ottawa, first to see the Great Lakes, first to reach Lake Superior (1621-23), and probably also Lake Erie (1625). He was fluent in Huron and acted as Champlain's interpreter, travelling with him. But he travelled even more widely on his own, south of the Great Lakes as well as north, even reaching the Atlantic coast on one journey. In 1616, Brûlé was captured by the Iroquois, who showered him with gifts and released him, hoping he would act as an ambassador of peace, but he seems to have made no effort in that direction. After twenty-three years living with the Indians, Brûlé was finally killed and eaten by Hurons of the Bear totem. Exactly why has never been explained, but the Hurons themselves regarded it as a disgraceful act, and treated the minor chief they believed responsible for the murder as a pariah.

cheveux relevés

Another young man, Nicolas de Vignau, was sent in 1610 to winter with the Algonkins. He claimed to have visited Hudson Bay with them, and to have seen there the wreckage of an English ship whose crew had been killed in a fight with the Indians. The Algonkins said he was lying, and under interrogation he retracted his statement. Yet it is true that Thomas Button's expedition to look for Henry Hudson and find the Northwest Passage did lose a ship in the Bay in 1612.

In 1614, Champlain got new backing when the Company of Canada was organized and given the fur monopoly. Next year he visited Huronia, between Lake Simcoe and Georgian Bay, joined a Huron war party that crossed Lake Ontario, and was there defeated and slightly wounded in an at-

tack on an Iroquois village.

Southwest of Huronia, he visited a group of Ottawas whom he called *Cheveux Relevés* because they wore their hair in an upsweep "better combed than our courtiers . . . . "

English conquest

For eighteen years, Champlain spent his life alternately in the backwoods, trying to keep enough furs flowing into Quebec to insure the solvency of his companies – and in France, trying to get enough money and colonists to keep New France alive. It barely survived. By 1627, it was still pitiably small and surrounded by enemies: the Iroquois to the south and west, the English to the south and east. New France in that year had a population of 107. In New England and Newfoundland there were 2,100 planters, not to mention almost four thousand English fishermen. In view of the weakness of Champlain's colony, it is hardly surprising that the English decided to capture it and add its fur trade to their own valuable trade in fish, furs and tobacco.

In 1628, David Kirke and his four brothers, armed with a commission from Charles I, occupied Tadoussac and captured the supply fleet sent to relieve Quebec, leaving New France destitute. Champlain's colony survived that winter on game and wild roots and exhausted its ammunition. Next spring, the Kirkes returned with a larger fleet and called on Champlain to surrender, "knowing your miserable condition and inability to resist." The only terms the French could secure were safe conduct to France with their personal belongings. Two families willing to accept English rule remained at Quebec, and a few *coureurs de bois* stayed with the Indians. Over the next four years the Kirkes reaped a fortune in fish and furs.

Then, in the treaty signed in 1632, England returned Canada to France. The Kirkes remained il-

While some explorers were still trying to find a way around Canada, a different breed of person was trekking the country beyond the St. Lawrence Valley. Known as the coureurs de bois, *these young "toughs" adopted the customs and habits of the native people, ate their food, learned their various languages, and joined in their games and war. To the fur trading companies they were indispensable, and despite their maverick ways, they formed important liaisons with the Indians and mapped the interior.*

legally at Tadoussac for another year and captured another year's furs, then returned to England, where David was knighted. In 1637, he and some associates were granted a charter to Newfoundland, and in 1639, he took over the Ferryland colony, formerly operated by Lord Baltimore. The Ferryland colony thrived, but David Kirke himself died in prison in 1654, awaiting trial on a charge by Baltimore's heir that he had taken Ferryland by force of arms. If so, it was no more than Baltimore himself had done, having evicted the fishermen who were there before him.

In the end, the Kirkes returned to Ferryland not as governors but as planters. When the Dutch attacked Newfoundland in 1663, they found three families of Kirkes there with fourteen fishing boats and sixty-six sharemen. They had survived the fall of Charles I, had made peace with Cromwell (signing over all their lands to the government), and had become wealthy colonists under Charles II.

Christmas Day, 1635

For the last two years of his life, Champlain was allowed to return to his ravaged colony. He died at Quebec on Christmas Day, 1635. But others had taken up his work. One of the founders of New France, when it finally began to grow in 1634, was a doctor named Robert Giffard. He had been at Quebec before the Kirkes. Now he returned with his wife, seven tradesmen and their wives, and twenty children. Other family groups arrived independently. By 1641, they numbered about two hundred. Meanwhile the *coureurs de bois* were pushing westward. Jean Nicollet, who had lived with the Indians from the age of twenty, reached Lake Michigan in 1634, and the headwaters of the Mississippi in 1635.

French and English colonies were now well established. The real clash between them was yet to come.

In 1629, Louis Kirke forced Champlain and his starving settlers to surrender – the first English victory at Quebec. The tiny town looked nothing like this medieval fortress.

65

Backwoodsmen

Dressed in the buckskins of the Indians and the coureurs de bois, *Father François-Joseph le Mercier spent 20 years living among the Hurons and the Iroquois from 1635.*

Beyond the reaches of the law, the church and the state, life for the *coureurs de bois* and the itinerant missionaries was far different from that in the villages. "Vicious in character and much addicted to women" – that was how Samuel Champlain described Etienne Brûlé and Nicholas Marsolet. They were both young men when they came to New France. When fur trade officials realized that the only way to corner the market was to trace the pelts to the original trappers, Brûlé, Marsolet, Jean Nicollet and Nicholas de Vignau were commissioned for the work. At the same time, the Recollets and Jesuits too were sending out young priests, hopefully to convert the "heathen." But while both the *coureurs* and the "Blackrobes" had to adopt many of the habits of the Indians, the *coureurs* threw both body *and* soul into survival. According to Champlain and the Jesuit fathers, they "revelled in unrestrained debauchery and libertinism," eating meat on holy days, fathering children outside the sanctity of marriage, and indulging themselves in all sorts of "unspeakable acts." "They set a scandalous example," complained Father Le Caron, "committing abuses and a thousand kinds of vile deeds, even more than these miserable Savages." But like it or not, priests, explorers and company officials had to deal with them: only the *coureurs* knew the Indians' moods and languages.

"The French themselves, better educated and raised in the School of Faith, are becoming Savages for no better reason than that they live with the Savages."

Father Gabriel Sagard, 1632

"Let no one be astonished at these acts of barbarism. Before the faith was received in Germany, Spain or England, those nations were not more civilized."

Father Paul Le Jeune, 1632

Etienne Brûlé once tricked his Iroquois captors into releasing him by claiming to have brought on a thunderstorm. Some years later, after defecting to the English, he was killed and eaten by the Hurons. Marsolet, Nicollet and de Vignau managed to return to Quebec before suffering similar fates.

67

Hélène Boullé was just twelve years old when she was "given in marriage" to Samuel Champlain, a man 30 years older than she. By law they had to wait two years before they lived together, and two months after the wedding, Champlain was off again to New France. It wasn't until she was 22 that Hélène joined him at Quebec (above). Used to the easy life (her father was the King's secretary), she packed for France four years later.

CHAPTER SIX

Women in New France

*Tender, delicate girls, who fear a dusting
of snow in France, are not surprised here
to see mountains of it. Now a big and good
long winter . . . does them no damage but to
keep their appetites up.*

Relation, 1642

The first woman to leave an account of a winter in Canada was Marguerite de la Roque, niece of Roberval, the governor of New France appointed in 1541. She sailed with her uncle as a volunteer, but incurred his wrath by having an affair with a young man of the expedition whose name was not recorded. When ordered to stay apart, they continued to meet secretly, aided by Marguerite's old servant, Damienne, while Roberval spent three weeks at St. John's refitting and trading with the fishermen.

On the day they sailed to go northward into the Strait of Belle Isle, he discovered their duplicity. Perhaps, also, he knew that his niece was pregnant. In any event, he was so furious that he ordered the three of them to be marooned. This harsh punishment was not unusual, for Roberval had been given absolute power by the King over every member of the expedition.

At an island now identified as Fogo, near the northeast corner of Newfoundland, he sent them ashore with gear, guns and ammunition. Fogo is no desert island, but a hundred and fifty square

miles of hill and forest, well supplied with water and game and in the finest fishing grounds. Since it was on the route of the French and Basque fishing fleets, there was a good chance that they would be rescued and returned to France. But no ship appeared and they began desperately preparing for winter.

Marguerite soon learned to work with her hands, using tools and guns. They built a log cabin lined with spruce boughs for bedding, and collected stocks of berries and game, curing and stretching the hides for clothes and blankets. But like most early settlers, they underestimated the Canadian winter. The food ran out. The young man fell sick. Around the first of March he died – probably of scurvy. Then Marguerite's baby was born.

By now she was a good hunter, and the ice floes brought food. Among other game she shot a polar bear – not uncommon around Fogo in the spring, when they arrive with drift ice, hunting seals. But in spite of her success as a hunter, her baby died that autumn, and not long afterwards, her old servant. She buried them beside her lover and set out resolutely to survive her second winter alone. It was nearly a year later before she was rescued by a French fishing ship, two years and five months after the voyage had begun.

Versions of her story were published in the 1550s by Marguerite d'Angoulème, Queen of Na-

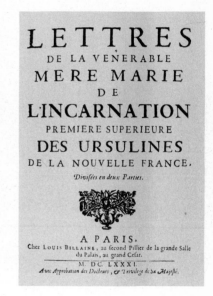

A penniless widow at 19 with an infant son, Marie Guyart ran her brother-in-law's business seven years, until her mystical religious experiences led her to enter the Ursuline convent at Tours. In 1639, a "vision" brought her to Canada, where she managed the financial and spiritual affairs of the Order and wrote approximately 13,000 letters.

Goaded into an unhappy first marriage for money, Marie-Madeleine de la Peltrie inherited both her husband's and father's fortunes when they died. Though she never took the vows herself, she accompanied the first Ursulines and nurses to New France and financed most of their work.

varre, and by the geographer André Thevet. Thus, the story became known to literate Frenchwomen of succeeding generations, and perhaps provided inspiration for the better-known ladies who followed her: Madame de la Peltrie, wealthy patron of the Ursulines, Marie de l'Incarnation, founder of the religious order at Quebec, and Jeanne Mance, co-founder of Montreal.

a dramatic conversion

Marie de l'Incarnation was born Marie Guyart, daughter of a master baker in Tours, in 1599. She had religious visions as a child, and by the age of fourteen understood her vocation. When she was seventeen, her family forced her to marry, much against her will. Two years later her husband died and left her with a six-month-old son.

Her visions now returned, stimulated by solitude and religious reading, and she experienced a dramatic conversion. Though a true mystic, she also had a practical gift for business, and five years after her husband's death was manager of a large carting firm owned by her brother-in-law.

Eight years later she entered an Ursuline convent, leaving her son with her sister. Again her visions continued. She saw a strange land which God revealed to her as Canada, where she was to "build a house for Jesus and Mary," with the help of a "Great Friend" to assist her in her work. In 1636, she met Madame de la Peltrie and recognized her at once as the companion of the vision.

Marie-Madeleine de la Peltrie, born in 1603, came from a wealthy and noble family. Her father, having no son, insisted on aristocratic unions for his daughters. So Marie-Madeleine, though she had hoped to take the veil, was forced into marriage at the age of seventeen. She was released from this unhappy state at twenty-two when her husband died, leaving her with a large fortune. Her family went to court to try to get control of her estates, but she won her case, and by the time she met Marie de l'Incarnation, she was the unchallenged mistress of great wealth which she wanted to devote to Christian works among Indian girls in New France. One of her estates was transferred in trust to the Ursulines, and she set off to find a ship to take herself, a young companion named Charlotte Barré, Marie, two other Ursulines and three nursing sisters, to Canada.

She chartered a ship, loaded it with supplies and furnishings to the value of eight thousand livres, and on August 1, 1639, the eight women landed at Quebec. Within three years, the la Peltrie fortune had erected a stone convent, ninety-two feet by twenty-eight, three storeys high, by far the most imposing structure in Canada at the time.

Madame de la Peltrie was immediately popular with the young Indian girls, and Marie and the other Ursulines tried their best to teach them. The convent was always filled, but remarkably few of the children ever became Christians. "Of a hundred girls who have passed through our hands, we have scarcely civilized one," Marie lamented in her old age. In the end the teaching convent, like the hospital founded by the sisters, became a mission not to the Indians but to the French settlers.

yet another missionary

Two years after the Ursulines, yet another visionary arrived at Quebec with another mission. This was Jeanne Mance, one of the ablest women of her age, come to found a hospital, not in some safe and defensible place like Quebec or Tadoussac, but at Montreal, then uninhabited, a hundred miles up the river, and not far north of the country of the Iroquois.

Jeanne's scheme had started with a religious organization, La Société Notre-Dame de Montréal, which quickly converted itself into a commercial company and took out a charter in 1640.

Canada's first schoolmistress, Marguerite Bourgeoys left behind the cloistered nun's life at 20 and came to Montreal in 1653. She built the first church there, acted as match-maker between local bachelors and the "King's Daughters," and once trekked to Quebec alone on snowshoes.

There were only two hundred people living at Quebec in 1639, when Madame de la Peltrie, Charlotte Barre (her travelling companion), three Ursuline nuns, and three nursing sisters arrived. After unpacking their next year's provisions, everyone rolled up the sleeves of their dresses and habits and set to work: tending gardens, putting up food, building, fixing, mending, baking . . . When fire destroyed the convent three years later, they simply rebuilt it.

Jeanne Mance was its eighth member. She was the only woman, but she immediately showed the qualities that would serve New France so well. After a meeting with her wealthy friend, Madame de Bullion, she announced that she had secured the funds to found her hospital, and turned her attention to lining up support for the colony. Before leaving France, she had enlisted the support of the royal family, and had increased the company's membership to forty-five, most of them wealthy investors.

instant dislike

She sailed from La Rochelle on May 9, 1641, the only woman in two shiploads of emigrants. On reaching Quebec, she met the Superior of the Ursuline convent and disliked her at once. Perhaps it was inevitable that two such strong-willed women as Jeanne and Mother Marie should disagree, but Jeanne's most outrageous act was to entice Madame de la Peltrie to leave the Ursulines and join the Montreal colony.

Marie and Governor Montmagny combined forces to discourage the plan to colonize Montreal. Much better to reinforce Quebec, they argued, and found their hospital on the nearby Île d'Orléans. But the colonists refused to be moved. Somebody christened them the "mad Montrealers," and by this name they were known that autumn.

They received no official help at Quebec, but found a friend in an old seigneur, Pierre de Puiseaux, who turned over his farm, two houses and dock to them, providing them with a headquarters of their own. Jeanne moved into one of the houses and Madame de la Peltrie moved in with her, taking along the convent furniture.

Though relations remained strained, the Quebec governor eventually agreed to assist the mad Montrealers and accompanied them to the island the following spring. Paul de Chomedey, Sieur de Maisonneuve and first governor of Montreal, landed there on May 17, 1642, with forty colonists to found the first permanent inland settlement in Canada.

Since Montreal was on the frontier exposed to Iroquois attack, their first undertaking was to build a fort. Twelve recruits from France joined them that autumn, bringing the total population to fifty-two. Fortunately it was a full year before the Iroquois decided to attack. Even then, it was a mere skirmish between scouting parties, in which three colonists were killed and three captured. One of the three escaped and warned Montreal to get its defences ready.

Meanwhile, the river had done its best to evict them. An ice blockade the first winter caused the St. Lawrence to flood the settlement. In their desperation they vowed to set up a cross on the summit of Mount Royal should the flood recede. Sure enough, it did, and on January 6, 1643, Maisonneuve and Jeanne led a procession to plant the cross on the summit.

martyrs

Jeanne's first hospital was finished that year, with a stable and chapel inside its stockade. The hospital treated both whites and Indians, especially those wounded in conflicts with the Indians. It was financially secure, for Madame de Bullion had endowed it for life, but the rest of the colony was not. To save it from bankruptcy, Jeanne had to spend a year in France drumming up support.

Her great powers of persuasion won new funds from former patrons, and she also managed to reorganize the Montreal Company under a new director and a new charter. But when she returned, she found the colony threatened from another direction. The Iroquois raids had turned into true warfare, the Hurons had been totally defeated, and the French settlements were in danger of be-

Jeanne Mance
Mademoiselle de l'Hôtel-Dieu

The second of twelve children, orphaned at age 20, Jeanne Mance gained her first experience as a nurse in her home town, Langres, during the Thirty Years' War. In 1640, she heard about the medical and missionary work of the women in New France, and at once felt "the call" to join them. Through acquaintances she met Angélique de Bullion, a woman of mystery and wealth, who had been interested in funding a hospital in New France. In May 1641, with a purse of over 40,000 *livres*, Jeanne set sail in the company of 13 men, and a year later joined Maisonneuve and Mme. de la Peltrie in the founding of Montreal. Soon after the Hôtel-Dieu was completed, the Iroquois launched their campaigns to destroy the settlement, and the hospital became the busiest place in town. Jeanne Mance worked through years of war and died in 1673.

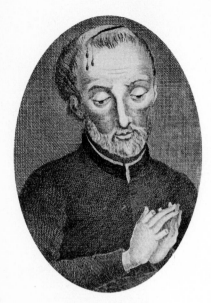

**Isaac Jogues
The First Martyr**

The first Jesuit priest murdered in New France, Isaac Jogues was 29 when he arrived as a missionary to the Hurons, and was appointed by Father Jean de Brébeuf to oversee the building of the Sainte-Marie mission on Georgian Bay. In 1642, he was captured by the Mohawks, forced to watch the slow death of a companion, Réne Goupil, and somehow endured the grisliest tortures ever recorded in history. With the aid of the Dutch, he escaped and returned to France. (An indult from the Pope was required so he could celebrate Mass — his fingers had been cut off, and he couldn't hold the Host during Communion.) The fact that Jogues returned to try to convert the Mohawks, tells a great deal about his character. Of all the Jesuits, he alone seems to have courted martyrdom. In the fall of 1646, he was recaptured, tortured and killed by an axe blow to the head.

ing overrun. Already the first martyrs at Sainte-Marie Among the Hurons had died in the flames.

The founding of this settlement back in 1639, nearly a thousand miles by river and portage from Quebec, is one of the early Jesuit ventures that in retrospect is hard to comprehend. The Jesuits had arrived when Quebec was reopened to the French in 1632. Seven years of evangelism among the Indians followed without a single convert. So they decided to move into the heart of Huron territory. Since the Hurons were already suspicious of the whites, being forced to accept them by the necessities of trade, the priests planted their fortified village near the shore of Lake Huron, garrisoned it with volunteers and stocked it with cows, pigs and chickens.

Five of the eighteen priests that had worked in the backwoods were killed — four by the Iroquois, one by the Hurons. Of the thirteen survivors who reached Quebec in 1650, eight immediately returned to France. Others, however, persisted. Three years later they actually established a mission at Onondaga, the Iroquois capital.

for God and the fur trade

Altogether, eight priests are known to have died at the hands of the Indians in New France, but whether they should all be called "martyrs" is a matter of opinion. One at least died in battle, and a number of them had been involved as military advisers. In any case, they died for the fur trade as truly as they died for God, and all the way from Tadoussac to Lake Huron, the cross and the brandy keg travelled together. It is true the Jesuits protested against the liquor trade, but their protests had no effect. Business was business, and far from objecting to the fur trade, they promoted it in every way possible, holding out the prospect of employment as guides, canoeists, and interpreters as an inducement to convert the Indians.

The Iroquois' destruction of Huronia backfired. Instead of capturing the fur trade, as they had hoped, they opened up the whole interior to the French. Fur traders now sent their own armed expeditions wherever they wished, to the north and west of the Great Lakes, and eventually down the Mississippi to Louisiana.

saved by a hair

After the Huron war, Montreal was under continuous siege. At one point its able-bodied defenders were reduced to seventeen. They were so desperate that Jeanne Mance, in a last-ditch effort to save the colony, urged the use of hospital funds to recruit mercenary soldiers. Maisonneuve went to France for that purpose, but while he was away, the Iroquois overran Trois-Rivières. Quebec and Montreal, with a mere handful of defenders, held out. He arrived back at Quebec on September 22, 1652, with 105 soldiers, saving New France by a hair's breadth. Under constant armed guard, a new and larger hospital was built at Montreal, and additional colonists were settled there.

Jeanne Mance served the colony for many years, and was its most powerful advocate in France, where she continued to have a miraculous knack for getting money, support, and volunteers. Among the settlers she brought out at her own expense was seventeen-year-old Etienne Truteau, ancestor of the entire Trudeau family, who married a girl from Montreal.

Despite repeated Iroquois attacks, the town flourished and grew. In 1660, seventeen Frenchmen who went to the Long Sault on the Ottawa River to ambush some Iroquois traders were surprised and besieged by a full-scale war party, held out for over a week, took a dreadful toll of the attackers, and so impressed the Iroquois that they were afraid to try capturing Montreal that year.

New France now had a population of nearly

three thousand, but suffered constant losses. An estimated seventy were killed or captured in 1661, and all farming outside the walls of the forts was stopped. But neither Quebec nor Montreal was ever abandoned. Maisonneuve was recalled to France in 1665, and the whole of Canada was placed under the governor of Quebec. Defences were strengthened, and there was intermittent peace.

Jeanne Mance continued, after Maisonneuve's departure, to bring out more colonists, advancing their passage money on loan. She also became godmother to more than seventy children born in the colony. By the time she died there in 1673, the town of which she was co-founder was the largest in Canada, with fifteen hundred people and an annual fur-market that drew eight hundred canoes from the interior.

Despite French rivalry with the Dutch businessmen of the Hudson, both the trade and the colonies flourished. Because they were established further north and had access by their own expeditions to the best fur country on the continent, the French reaped the lion's share of the fur trade.

the "Sun King's" domain

The town of Quebec was now the centre of a far-flung empire. Its authority had been extended not only over Montreal and the outposts to the west, but also over Acadia and southern Newfoundland, where the French had planted several small colonies and built the great fortress of Placentia. The Quebec governor had become the governor-general of New France; the "Sun King," Louis XIV, was on the French throne, dominating Europe; and his possessions in North America seemed to be secure. Except for a small part of the east coast of Newfoundland, the only English colonies north of Maine were the first posts opened by the Hudson's Bay Company in James Bay.

During an Indian raid on Ville-Marie (Montreal) in 1661, Mme. Celles Duclos saved the lives of Charles Le Moyne de Longeuil and the defenders by arriving with an armful of rifles.

Jean-Baptiste Colbert took charge of the affairs of New France in 1663, and was promptly nick-named "Monsieur du Nord" by the courtiers of Louis XIV. One of his first moves to build up the colonial population was to double the taxes and duties of bachelors over 18 years of age.

French society had been transplanted intact across the Atlantic, with its three estates: nobles, clergy and commoners. But in New France, nobility was relatively easy to attain, and many commoners rose to be nobles by the simple expedient of purchasing a *lettre d'anoblissement* out of the profits of the fur trade. Imported goods were in great demand, splendour of a sort was in vogue, and though God's work showed little sign of bearing fruit, the white population of New France was at least outwardly devout. Anyone who failed to attend Mass on Sunday was liable to find himself in the stocks at Quebec on Monday morning.

Government was soundly established, with a governor-general (always a professional soldier and a noble), and from 1663 on, an intendant, responsible for civil administration. From 1645 onward, there was an administrative council at Quebec, including clergy, government officials and elected members. It assumed some legislative powers, but as time passed came more and more to act as a court of appeal in judicial affairs.

a royal province

Finally, there was the bishop, first appointed in 1657. At first he was such a power in the land that governors were recalled on his complaint. From 1663, partly because of intervention and appeals from the Jesuits, Louis XIV took over the administration of New France himself, making it a royal province. He placed its administration in the hands of his trusted minister, Jean-Baptiste Colbert, under whom the colonizing effort was to reach its zenith.

Quebec, 1670

The 1667 census of New France placed 5,870 people in the colony, most of them settled along the St. Lawrence near the towns of Montreal, Trois-Rivières and Quebec. By this time most of the arable land on both sides of the river had been cleared, and farms were flourishing. In 1668, Intendant Jean Talon sent Colbert a note, telling him not to send any more cattle – 3,400 head were quite enough. In 1665, Talon had 14 stallions and mares (called "French moose" by the Indians) brought from France to ease the farmers' labour. Under protection – a 200-*Livres* fine for mistreatment – the horse population had risen to 100 by 1672. Other industries, too, were growing. Shoes and hats were fashioned in cottage-tanneries; cloth and linen were woven from sheep's wool and home-grown flax; and a brand new brewery churned out over 2,000 kegs of beer in its first year of operation. The first acres of pine, oak and spruce were felled and the timber floated down rivers, marked for Montreal's sawmill and foreign markets. Under Talon's supervision Quebec literally became the first Canadian "boom-town."

Looking east along the St. Lawrence, this 1670 aerial view shows the town of Quebec (bottom) and surrounding farmlands on the Ile d'Orleans and river's edge. Tiny habitant *cottages cluster around the seigneurial manors, and windmills and church spires suggest the beginnings of a skyline. The waterway is busy with ships loaded with furs returning to France for more immigrants.*

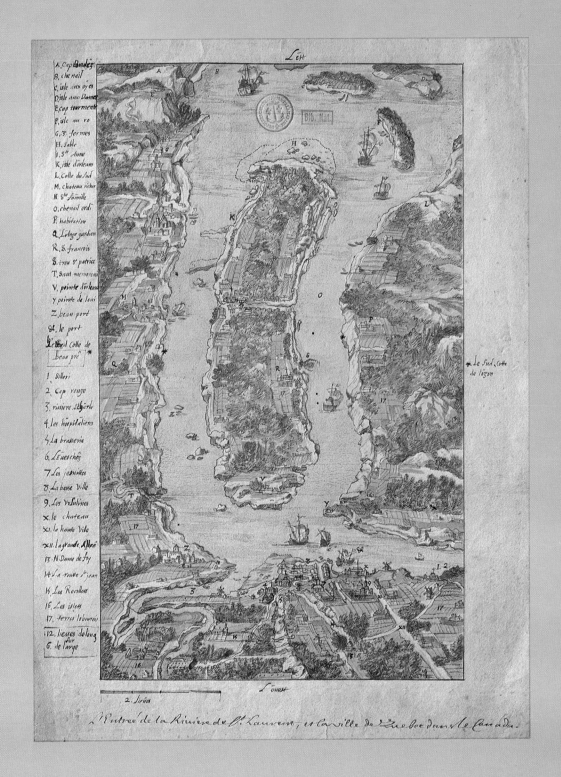

Black Robes and Nuns

The early history of the Church in Canada is documented with remarkable drama and colour in two extraordinary paintings from the mid-1600s. Below, the deaths of ten Christians are combined into one composite, showing the tortures by the Indians who held the "Black Robes" responsible for epidemics that ravaged their nations. Opposite, four corner-miniatures and the centre panel document the work of the first nursing and teaching sisters brought to Canada by Mme. de la Peltrie.

Abbé Hugues Pommier's The Jesuit Martyrs *(1665) combines the separate deaths of the early missionaries into one tale of horror: (foreground, left to right): Isaac Jogues and two companions; Lalement and Brébeuf; (background) Noël Chabanel; Anne de Noüe; Joseph Onahare, an Algonkin convert; Charles Garnier and Antoine Daniel.*

Built in 1642, the Ursuline Convent became a social, religious and educational centre of Quebec. On the grande allée, *the colony's governor l'Ailleboust and Trois-Rivières' governor Bochart are out for a ride on horseback. Mme. de la Peltrie chats with an Indian in front of the gatehouse as Jérôme Lalement, the superior of missions, approaches. Mother Marie de l'Incarnation (top right) and Mother St-Athanase (top left) conduct classes.*

Under the watchful eyes of chaperones, churchmen and the rakish glances of a few notorious bachelors, the "King's Daughters" arrived, looking for husbands.

CHAPTER SEVEN

The King's Daughters

The reason they marry so easily in that country is the difficulty of making contact with persons of the opposite sex. A man has to speak of marriage . . . otherwise slander comes to haunt one and the other.

Baron Lahontan, *Nouveaux Voyages,* 1703

Shortly after Louis XIV assumed control of the government of France at the age of twenty-two, he took New France out of the hands of private individuals and established what has come to be known as "the Royal Régime." Canada became a French province, and the king and his chief minister, Jean-Baptiste Colbert, set out to build it up and make it pay dividends to the Crown.

History characterizes Colbert as a great administrator – but he was also ruthless and strongly anti-clerical. He regarded the second estate, the clergy, as a group of parasites, and made every effort to build up the bourgeoisie, the emerging merchant class, at Church expense. Bishop Laval remained a member of the council at Quebec, but Colbert instructed the intendant – his personal appointee – to do all in his power to keep the bishop from actually sitting in on the meetings.

At the same time, Colbert built up the secular power by creating the intendant's office. The man he named to the post, Jean Talon, was a true Colbert disciple, with strong mercantile bias, a friend to trade, commerce and small business of every kind. He was diplomatic enough to keep his anti-clericalism concealed and won the admiration of church leaders while curbing their powers.

One of his first acts was to build up the population of Canada by bringing in new settlers, especially women settlers. For the French population of Quebec still consisted mainly of unmarried males, many of whom interbred freely with the Indians, "wasting their seed among the pagans" instead of increasing the strength of the colony.

Some of Talon's first settlers were families, who were offered land in new villages along the St. Lawrence. He had seized the land from absentee landlords who had done nothing to develop it, then shared it out in pie-shaped pieces centring on a village where the houses were to be clustered together for defence. Each settler-family was required to clear two acres for itself and two for a future immigrant.

The plan worked, but not fast enough. After consultation with the King, Talon began bringing out shiploads of "King's Daughters" as wives for unmarried settlers and French soldiers, who were encouraged to remain at Quebec and accept grants of land after their term of service had expired. Four hundred and three demobilized soldiers took land grants in 1666, and there were many others in succeeding years.

The term King's Daughters (*filles du roi*) was originally applied to orphan girls raised in France

Orphan girls, daughters of debtors, streetwalkers and runaway wives – these were the women recruited by Louis XIV's chief administrators to become the wives of soldiers and bachelor settlers in New France. Even if the term "King's Daughters" seems hardly fitting, these thousand or so women served their purpose – by 1670 the population was soaring.

**Marie-Madeleine de Verchères
A Textbook Heroine**

Every Canadian schoolbook reader
knows about the heroics of the
15-year-old girl, Madeleine de
Verchères: how she outran a band
of Iroquois to her father's fort,
closed the gates, signalled nearby reinforcements, and frightened
off the invaders single-handedly.
Madeleine was the fourth of 12
children. Her father was one of
the soldiers who had come to New
France with the Salières régiment;
her mother was a peasant girl, just
twelve and a half years old when
she married. Two years before young
Madeleine made her historic dash to
safety, her mother had fended off
a similar attack. One of her brothers
and two brothers-in-law were killed.
What happened to Madeleine? At 28,
she married a bad-tempered land-
owner, was in and out of court over
quarrels with neighbors, and became
the brunt of off-colour burlesques
written by Abbé Gervais Lefebvre.

in state-run institutions. To these girls the King stood *in loco parentis*, having the same legal relationship as a father to his daughters. But the King's Daughters brought to New France by Talon were not all orphans by any means. Many of them were volunteers from peasant villages, some of them street girls escaping to what they hoped was a better life, and a few even proved to be married women trying to escape intolerable husbands.

the King's dowry

The King's Daughters arrived in annual shipments from 1665 to 1671, a hundred to a hundred and fifty girls each year, more than eleven hundred of them in all. Besides her personal qualities, and whatever small property she might possess, each girl brought with her a dowry from the King: an ox, a cow, two pigs, two chickens, two barrels of salt beef, and eleven crowns in cash—no small endowment for a man who had already received his land grant and cleared his minimum four acres.

Though the girls were not forced into marriage, the transaction had an atmosphere of an auction. On landing in Quebec, they were separated into three groups and sent to separate sheds for inspection, where interested men might look them over and be questioned, in their turn, about their suitability as husbands. But a girl who was asked rarely refused. She was married on the spot by priests and notaries standing by for the purpose, then bundled off with her new husband to find out what she had got herself into. Once married, she had no recourse. She was her husband's property. She could never get a divorce, and could not get a separation unless he beat her with a stick thicker than his wrist.

Talon took a great interest in this breeding program, and made every effort to find husbands for even the least-promising brides. But there were a few that even he could not match—fifteen out of the first hundred and fifty—who wound up in domestic service. The year after their arrival, Talon reported to the King on the state of the brides' fertility—most were already pregnant, he rejoiced. By 1670, the birthrate was phenomenal, with almost seven hundred new children being born each year among a population of 4,500. At that rate the population would double every six years.

Even this did not satisfy Talon or the King. He made a law against bachelors: parents who failed to marry their daughters by the age of sixteen or their sons by the age of twenty were fined. Single men who failed to marry within two weeks of the arrival of a shipment of King's Daughters were forbidden to fish, hunt or engage in the fur trade. Family allowances, of a sort, were instituted. Couples with ten children could claim a pension of 300 livres a year—400 if they had twelve. Such families were not at all unusual.

tenant farmers

The people who farmed the seigneuries—many of them vast tracts of virgin forests—were tenants, and the terms on which they held their sub-titles varied from one seigneur to another, but the payments were very low: perhaps a pint of corn per acre, and four days' work yearly on roads, bridges or mills, or on the seigneur's farm. A tenant who failed to clear and plant his land was liable to eviction.

The oldest seigneuries were in Acadia, where the Poutrincourt grant in the Annapolis Valley was farmed successfully from 1610 to 1614, and where Poutrincourt's son, Jean de Biencourt, continued to maintain a colony without assistance from France until his death in 1623. The first Quebec seigneur to establish permanent habitants on his land was Robert Giffard, who was granted Beauport, northeast of the citadel, in 1634. The

Fashions of New France

All the gentlemen are wearing full-bottomed wigs, pointed low-heeled shoes, silk hose, knee-breeches, and close-coats underneath shorter surcoats; the woman, curtsying to the man's bow, has her hair in ringlets and wears a tight-bodiced, floor-length dress with puffed and slashed sleeves. Although the artist has shown these 1660's arrivals in Quebec in the Paris fashions of the day, the average Quebecker probably dressed in less-elegant style.

At the top of Jean Talon's list of ambitious plans for New France was the creation of a ship-building industry. Before he returned to France in 1672, he had supervised the building of a 120-ton barque, two 300-ton timber ships called flûtes, and had begun construction of an 800-ton ship and smaller vessels.

term "*habitant*" is now almost equivalent to the English "inhabitant," but in early Quebec it was a title conferring status. It distinguished the landholder from the casual labourer, and was the second grade in the social hierarchy, roughly equivalent to "citizen" in Greece and Rome.

Though *habitants* were tenants, they could buy and sell their holdings just like freehold land, and there was nothing to prevent an *habitant* farmer from building up his original grant into a great estate, as some of them proceeded to do. Much commoner, however, was subdivision of the land among heirs, and further subdivision in succeeding generations, until the original grant was cut into narrow strips, each with a tiny bit of river-front – a system followed because access to the river, for fishing and transport, was all-important in early times.

When seigneuries were sold they were subject to a sales tax of twenty per cent. When *habitant* holdings were sold, they were taxed at twelve per cent. So the government collected substantial revenues on land transactions, particularly when seigneuries were subdivided into towns and villages.

security for all time

Very large seigneuries were held by the Church, by the missions, and by the religious orders. Bishop Laval collected seigneuries throughout his lifetime, until a quarter of all the *habitants* in the Quebec region were his tenants. He refused to sell or alienate any part of this property, but left it in trust to the schools that he founded, thus making them financially secure for all time to come.

When the Carignan regiment was disbanded at Quebec in 1666, and more than half the demobilized soldiers chose to remain, all the officers were granted seigneuries on condition that they take on their men as *habitants*.

The island of Montreal was originally a single seigneury, but this was small by the standards of the time. Some grants extended southeastward from the St. Lawrence River right to the Atlantic coast and included huge strips of Acadia, where the *habitants* paid a tiny tax to absentee landlords in Quebec. The practice continued even when Acadia passed into English hands. The largest original grant had a hundred and eighty miles of river front, but was soon enlarged by absorbing two neighbouring seigneuries. Such unwieldy private kingdoms might have become equivalent to the dukedoms of medieval Europe had they lasted, but they did not. Most of them were quickly subdivided and sold for profit by landlords who had never laid eyes on a square foot of Canada.

absolute power

Talon, who came as close as anyone in the new world to wielding absolute power, simply confiscated undeveloped seigneuries by the stroke of a pen (he had the backing of an absolute monarch), then parcelled them out to new seigneurs who he hoped would develop them. Many of these men were a disappointment, but at least most of them stayed in the colony, covering their failures as landlord-farmers by engaging, often without licence, in the fur trade. The sons of such seigneurs sometimes became *coureurs de bois*, in defiance of a law conceived by Colbert forbidding this occupation. French settlers were to remain at home practising trades, professions and agriculture.

Talon's land-settlement schemes succeeded for all that. A land census of 1667 showed about eleven thousand acres under cultivation. In 1668 there were fifteen thousand. By that time, Quebec had over three thousand head of cattle (almost as many cows as people), but only eighty-five sheep.

During Talon's intendancy, Louis de Buade, Comte de Frontenac, was sent from France as

**Jean Talon
The King's Bachelor**

At a time when France's prospects for success in America seemed most grim, Louis XIV sent a 29-year-old bachelor to Quebec to see if the past century's exploration and work could be salvaged. An administrative genius, full of brilliant ideas and schemes, Jean Talon arrived in 1665. In just five years, France claimed sovereignty over three-fourths of the continent. It was his idea to bring over the *filles du roi* as brides for single settlers, and to his credit must go the first sawmill, brewery, shipyard, tannery, textile factory, coal mine . . . and the first planned town. What didn't he establish? When he retired in poor health in 1672, New France suffered a major setback. The King kept him on as personal secretary, colonial counsel and royal wardrobe advisor (Talon was always a natty dresser). He died at 68, a bachelor.

**François de Laval
The King's Bishop**

He was a Montmorency – the family claiming to be the first barons of France. He was proud, powerful and catholic in his beliefs, and for 50 years he quarrelled with governors, intendants, councils and parishioners over the powers of Church and State. François de Laval was named in 1657 to lead the Church in North America, not by the archbishop of Rouen, as had been the tradition, but by the Pope himself on the recommendation of the Jesuits. Laval's first five years at Quebec were marked by open squabbling for Church control. In 1663, Louis XIV finally ended the dispute and named him Bishop of New France and number two man in the Sovereign Council troika. He staunchly opposed the use of liquor in trade; reluctantly accepted the governor's reduction in tithes; and often locked horns with religious community leaders before he died at age 85. He was founder of Laval U.

governor-general. He remained relatively quiet until Talon's departure in 1672, then tried to take the government into his own hands, and almost wrecked New France in the process. He feuded fiercely with the fur traders, with the Jesuits, and with Talon's successor, Jacques Duchesneau, who was appointed in 1675.

These feuds were exceedingly bitter. Frontenac accused the Jesuits of enriching themselves in the fur trade, of being hypocrites, of revealing the secrets of the confessional, and of perverting the minds of the people from their loyalty to the state. The Jesuits fought back by accusing Frontenac not only of being involved in the fur trade for private gain, but of conspiring to create a monopoly, of intercepting church mail, and of being bitterly anti-clerical.

In his feud with the intendant, Frontenac accused Duchesneau of being in league with the Jesuits, of secretly enriching himself in the fur trade, and of being incompetent for his office. At the height of this feud, Bishop Laval returned from a long visit to France and got embroiled on the side of the intendant against the governor. After doing immense damage to the colony, Frontenac was finally recalled in 1682. When he was reappointed seven years later, he had more important business than fighting with other officials, and began to show the great military aptitude for which he is remembered.

Indian morals be damned

One of his most controversial policies was that of trading brandy to the Indians. It had been going on for a long time, despite official condemnation. Two young men had been hanged, at the instigation of the Church, for trading brandy only a few years before, and a third had been flogged. But Frontenac insisted it was the patriotic duty of fur traders to compete with the English on their own

terms. It was no more illegal to sell liquor to the Indians, he said, then it was to sell it to the Dutch. In 1678, he summoned representatives of the three estates to discuss the issue. Christened "the Brandy Parliament," this meeting sided with Frontenac by a vote of fifteen to five. The sentiments of most of the colony were undoubtedly with him. Indian morals be damned. The brandy trade flourished.

the old order passes

The result of the Frontenac disorders was a reform of the machinery of government. Louis XIV was forced to define and limit the powers of the governor, the intendant, and the officials who served under them, and to separate the powers of church and state. Under the system that prevailed in New France from that time forward, the government remained autocratic, but it was orderly. And on the whole, it was fair.

While the internal feuds were going on, and the partisans of the governor, the intendant and the bishop were fighting in the streets, the successful colonization continued. The shipments of King's Daughters ceased after 1671 – presumably because a fair balance between the sexes had been achieved – but the flow of families went on.

At the village level, government was exercised by captains of militia who were *habitants*, not seigneurs, and who answered not to the landlords, but directly to the government in Quebec. From 1669 onward, all *habitants* served in militia companies organized by parishes, mustered for training after the harvest was in, ready to be called up by the seigneur in case of war. Though they drew no pay and had no civil appointments, the captains of these companies transmitted government orders directly to the villagers and reported their grievances. It was a simple and effective system that bypassed the parish priest, formerly the *de facto* chief

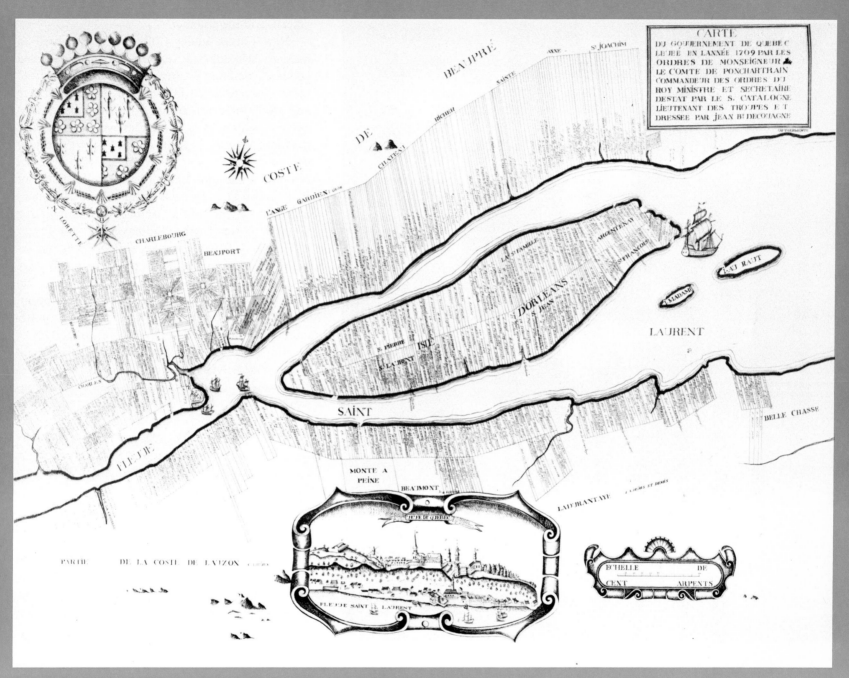

This 1709 seigneurial map of the area surrounding Quebec shows the settlement pattern in the St. Lawrence Valley. Before roads, the river was Main Street, with tenants' houses along the shore and farms extending in strips to the wilderness. Under Talon attempts were made to redesign seigneuries, clustering workers' cottages around the fortified manor house (see Charlesbourg and Beauport above). Planned as a defence measure, it also kept the habitants in check.

Anne de La Grange, known for her rare beauty, haughtiness and biting wit, secretly married Comte Frontenac in 1648, and the two quickly managed to squander their fortunes through high living. Bankrupt, Frontenac obtained the post of governor of Canada, and until he was recalled in 1682, played the tyrant, seeking wherever possible his own and his associates' benefit. In France, Madame Frontenac played her own role, explaining away rumours of his wrongdoings.

official, and the seigneur.

New France under Colbert was supposed to become self-sufficient except for manufactured goods. Agriculture greatly expanded, fishing settlements were founded in the Gulf of St. Lawrence and along the south coast of Newfoundland, timber and shipbuilding industries were begun, and the first brewery was opened. But Colbert's grandiose plans for ships of 500 tons came to nothing. No one at the time knew how to build a ship of that size, in any case, but small shipyards launching vessels a tenth of that tonnage began operating all the way from Quebec to Placentia.

To serve these industries Colbert sent out indentured workers, signed up for terms of five years, after which they could, if they chose, become *habitants*. None of his colonists were criminals. "It is important to plant good seed," he declared. But they were not all French, either. One of his ships brought a mixture of Germans, Portuguese, Hollanders, and even Algerians. Altogether, the immigrants numbered approximately ten thousand, of whom nearly four thousand were indentured workers. Those who were required to stay sometimes married English colonists, and many slipped across undefended and ill-defined borders into the promised lands of Virginia and New England.

By the end of the seventeenth century, French colonization was at an end and French subsidies had practically dried up, but the colony was now able to flourish on its own. Its revenues consisted only of the sales taxes on land, an import duty on wines and spirits, and a stiff export tax on fur, but these revenues were enough for the simple requirements of the colonial government. Fur trading, farming, and incomes from seigneuries not only kept officials solvent, but sometimes made them moderately wealthy. The wars that were to ruin New France were still far in the future.

House of Cards

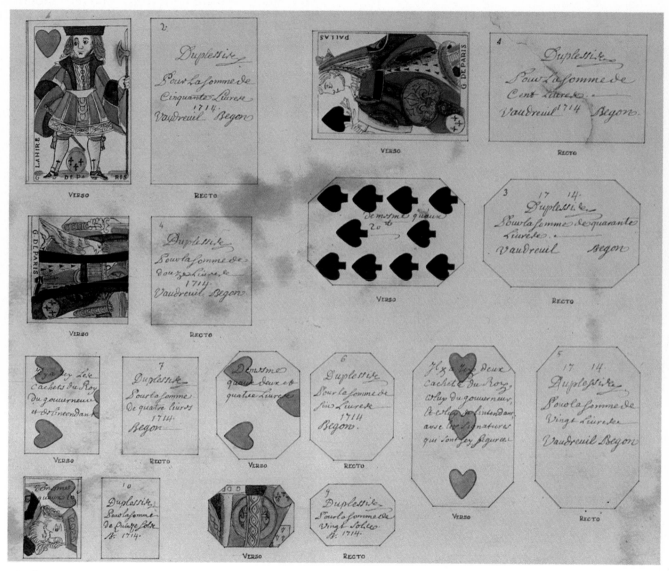

The first Canadian money was not issued in the form of gold or silver coins or paper currency but playing cards. Strange? Hardly, considering today's dollar bills, personal cheques and plastic credit cards. It was an ingenious idea for a time, concocted by Intendant Jacques de Meulles in 1685, when the soldiers had to be paid and the pay-ship was late arriving. Twenty-five years later, with prices soaring, Intendant Michel Bégon could only redeem card money at half its face-value.

The Four Kings

While the French and English were engaged in the ongoing struggle to claim the continent, the Indians were hardly sitting around waiting to hand over their territories to the white man. "We are born free!" said the Onondaga chief La Grande Guele to Governor La Barre, after the interim peace

Sayayouguaroughta, a Mohawk of the Bear clan, grandfather of Joseph Brant.

Honeeyeathtawnorow, called John, a sachem of the wolf clan.

of 1684 between the French and the Iroquois. But it took another hundred years of back-and-forth alliances before the tribes of the Great Confederacy finally laid down their arms. And in that time, neither the French nor the English were foolish enough to ignore the strength of the Iroquois.

In the end the English triumphed, almost certainly because they held the allegiance of most tribes of the St. Lawrence and the Great Lakes. The four portraits below were painted in London, where in 1710, these "Kings" were wined and dined by Queen Anne's ministers before signing peace with England.

Orontony, called Nicholas, a Huron of the Turtle clan, died in an epidemic.

Theyanoguin, called Hendrik, fell in battle at Crown Point in 1755.

Leaving Fort Frontenac (Kingston), the base of his fur trading operation, La Salle and a flotilla of Indian guides set out for the western shore of Lake Ontario. Threading his way through lakes and rivers, he found his way through the interior to the mouth of the Mississippi River in 1682.

CHAPTER EIGHT

Masterless Men

They smoke incessantly, singing the songs of their country, which they have learned from their fathers. . . . Every so often they disembark from their canoes and rest. . . . They calculate distances by the number of pipes they smoke.

Dispatch from Frontenac to Louis XIV, 1696

While the farms and towns of New France were being established under official patronage, the interior of the continent was being explored by outlaws. On rare occasions the explorers had licences to trade, even official commissions to establish posts as far to the west as possible, but more often they travelled through the wilderness at the risk of their lives and returned to the colonies at the risk of being fined, flogged, imprisoned or – if the law was truly enforced as it rarely was – hanged by the neck until dead.

The rewards for taking these risks had to be tempting. The occasional *coureur de bois* returned with a load of furs that made him temporarily wealthy, but like the much later freelance miner with his poke full of gold dust, he usually lost it all at the nearest house of pleasure.

As early as the 1660s, a few daring *coureurs* had reached the western tribes that lived on the Canadian Shield north and west of the Upper Lakes. Leaving Trois-Rivières by way of the Saint-Maurice, crossing the upper Ottawa, Jean Peré traded with the Ottawas north of Lake Huron in

1669 and reached the shores of Hudson Bay in 1684. He was captured by the Hudson's Bay Company and taken as a prisoner to England, but he returned to Quebec three years later.

Captured by the Iroquois at the age of fifteen or sixteen, Pierre-Esprit Radisson was adopted into the Mohawk nation and lived with them for some time. Eventually, however, he escaped to the Dutch outpost of Fort Orange (now Albany, New York), and returned to Trois-Rivières in 1654 by way of Holland and France. In 1657, he was back among the Iroquois as a volunteer with the Jesuit missionaries. Two years later he joined Médard Chouart des Groseilliers, to whom he was related by marriage, in a journey to Lake Superior, wintered there with the Sioux, and returned the next year by way of the Ottawa River. When they got back from this expedition, Radisson and Des Groseilliers were fined and imprisoned for trading without a licence.

For years Des Groseilliers had had the idea of voyaging to Hudson Bay by sea to establish the fur trade there. In 1662, he and Radisson left Montreal, announcing that they were making the trip. Instead, they slipped away to Boston. Three years later they were invited to London, where they began the negotiations that led to the chartering of the Hudson's Bay Company in 1670. From then until 1675, they led English expeditions into the bay, until they were persuaded to change their al-

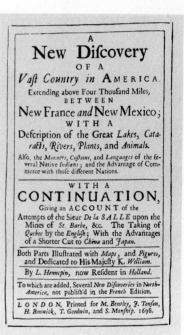

Called by some "the greatest liar" for his claim to have reached the Mississippi delta nearly two years before La Salle, Louis Hennepin spent the last years of his life writing books about his travels. His work, including the book A New Discovery, *though short on facts and high on exaggeration, was published in 46 editions and translated into several languages.*

legiance again, and returned to Quebec in 1676.

In 1682, they made a voyage for the Compagnie du Nord, organized by the governor and merchants of Quebec as an answer to the Hudson's Bay Company, and founded Fort Bourbon, the first post established by the company in Hudson Bay.

smuggling furs

On this voyage they captured a ship named the *Bachelor's Delight*, owned by a group of New Englanders, took her and her cargo of furs to Quebec as prizes, and landed her crew there as prisoners. The ship had been smuggling furs under the noses of the Gentlemen Adventurers, who held a royal monopoly on the English fur trade. But since England and France were at peace, the governor of Quebec released the prisoners and returned the ship to her owners.

This so outraged the two *coureurs* that they went off to France seeking redress, but the government there turned a deaf ear. Des Groseilliers swallowed his disappointment and went back to Trois-Rivières to engage in the legitimate fur trade, but Radisson deserted once more to the Hudsons' Bay Company and got possession of Fort Bourbon for them in 1684. It was renamed York Fort, and he spent the next three years there as superintendent of trade. He barely escaped being taken prisoner by the French in 1686, when they captured all the principal Hudson Bay posts (the first act of war in the long series of wars that were to follow). Had he fallen into French hands at that point, he would doubtless have ended his life on the gallows. Instead, he retired to England in 1687, took out citizenship, and lived as an English gentleman until 1710.

Few *coureurs* achieved such deeds of derring-do, but all shared equal dangers and greater hardships for scanty rewards and scantier fame. Jac-

Smoking was one of many habits the coureurs de bois *acquired from the Indians. Etienne Brûlé described the smoking mixture* kinikinik *as having "a taste most excellent" and its effect "enlivening as if with wine." Marc Lescarbot wrote of some Frenchmen so addicted to it "that they can no more do without it than without food or drink." Father Biard went as far as saying some* coureurs *"would sell their shirts from their backs to drink this smoke," and added, "the habit once acquired, one cannot be rid of it except with great difficulty."*

ques de Noyon, whose name has barely survived, discovered the route from Trois-Rivières to Rainy Lake and the Lake of the Woods in 1688. Though he reported his discovery, it was not followed up for almost twenty years.

Denis Riverin, writing in 1705, left a record of the typical journeys of these mostly nameless men, who by that time numbered some five hundred. He described them as young men (since age could not endure the hardships of their occupation), some from noble families, others the sons of *habitants*, and a few of no discernible background at all.

They travelled, as a rule, in threes, using canoes, which the French by this time could handle as expertly as any Indian. For some reason they never learned to build them, but got them in trade from the Indians. On still water, he said, they could cover forty-five miles a day, more when moving with the current. They poled up rivers that were too swift for paddling, and sometimes had to portage canoe, supplies and trade goods around impassable stretches two or three miles in length.

eating moccasins

The *coureurs* carried a tarpaulin that served as a sail when the wind was behind them, and as a crude tent. For supplies they took only a little biscuit, peas and corn. For trade goods they carried small kegs of brandy, some bolts of bright cloth, and a little hardware. They lived almost entirely on game and fish. They would set a small net whenever they were in camp, and usually had a good supply of fish in the morning. When they could not get fish and game, they resorted to eating reindeer moss and rock lichens. If really stuck for food on the return journey, they boiled the poorer skins from their stock of fur into a sort of glue which they ate. When desperate, they boiled and ate their moccasins. On these journeys they often travelled a thousand, and sometimes fifteen

A master of the backwoods' arts of deception and survival, Pierre-Esprit Radisson twice escaped from the Indians by trickery. Before he died in England at age 70, he had worked as an interpreter for the Dutch, penetrated to the far shore of Lake Superior for the French, established fur posts in the Hudson Bay region for both the French and the English, and served five years as the first wintering partner for the HBC – a man with no master but himself.

95

Temperamental, suspicious, arrogant, hated by his partners and crew, Robert Cavelier de La Salle met his end in a swamp off the Gulf of Mexico while trying to relocate the mouth of the Mississippi. Two years later, pursued by justice, the murderers killed each other off.

hundred miles up-country.

A canoe could carry trade goods worth 3,500 livres, which could be exchanged for twice that value in beaver pelts, says Riverin. But by his time the competition for beaver pelts was keen, and so many of them had been brought in by the small army of *coureurs* that the price was beginning to fall.

dissolute living

Since they required little time for actual trade, they revelled in dissolute living, sleeping, smoking, drinking brandy, gambling, and seducing the wives and daughters of the Indians. They lived much the same way when they got back to Montreal. Gambling, drinking and wenching often consumed the entire profits of a voyage, Riverin reported. He added that the *coureurs de bois* lived in complete independence, accounting to no one for their actions, acknowleding no superior, no judge, no law, no police, no subordination.

No wonder the rigid and hierarchical society of Louis XIV's New France found them hard to accept. But in spite of being odious and socially offensive, arriving in Montreal or Trois-Rivières, ragged and barefoot with six months' growth of hair and a thirst for brandy and girls, the *coureurs* were absolutely essential to the economy of the country. They were the boys who brought in the pelts on which the fur traders grew wealthy, and on which the government collected its revenues. Practically the whole colony conspired to protect them from the law, and when they were haled before a judge, he refused to sentence them to prison or the gallows, but fined them and turned them loose to continue the trade that kept New France alive.

The English had nothing similar to the *coureurs de bois*. Nearest to it were the masterless men of Newfoundland – unemployed fishermen or deserters from King's ships who took to the woods. At least in one case, under a leader named Peter Kerrivan, they formed themselves into an organized band of outlaws. But the masterless men of Newfoundland did little for the trade or development of the country. They opened up travel routes and built some of the first crude roads, and eventually settled some of the more remote outports. Compared to the *coureurs de bois* of Quebec, they left no mark on history.

The English, established close to the best trapping lands of North America, followed a different system. They built posts on the shore of Hudson Bay, fortified them, staffed them with men who had no experience in the woods, and waited for the Indians to bring in their furs. It is true that Henry Kelsey, one of the few Englishmen ever to attempt a life similar to that of the *coureurs*, went out as a youth to Hudson Bay in 1684 and made long journeys of exploration. Kelsey became the first white man to reach the prairies, but his work was never followed up by travelling traders, as happened in New France. The Hudson's Bay Company did not begin to trade inland until it was forced to do so by competition from Montreal.

Kelsey's greatest achievement

Kelsey helped to establish the first Churchill River post, but his greatest achievement was a journey from Hudson Bay to the Saskatchewan River in 1690. He returned in 1692, having achieved his main purpose: diverting the furs from the far west down the Churchill and neighbouring river systems to the posts on Hudson Bay. He rose to become deputy governor of York Factory, and in 1718 governor of all the Bay posts.

On Hudson Bay, the English had the great advantage of being right on the estuaries of major rivers down which the Indians could bring their furs with ease and in perfect security. They did not

One of the most itinerant men of the cloth, Father Louis Hennepin spent two years as missionary at Fort Frontenac (Kingston) and then accompanied La Salle to Niagara. Captive among the Sioux in 1680, he buried his chalice and vestments and joined in the hunt.

Prince Rupert—cousin of Charles II of England (etc., etc.): for two hundred years, two-thirds of Canada bore his name, Rupert's Land. Although he never set foot on the continent, in 1670 he became titular head of the new Hudson's Bay Company and governor of all lands draining into the Arctic and Pacific oceans and the Mississippi. The HBC still holds some of the land today.

have to pass through or near the lands of unfriendly tribes, and this became especially important after the French had rashly renewed the war with the Iroquois in 1684. But the French forces were laid low by disease before a shot was fired, and the expedition ended in a peace conference.

In 1687, the French mounted a full-scale invasion under the Marquis de Denonville. During this attack the principal villages of the Senecas were all ransacked and burned. The Iroquois replied in the only way they could. They took Fort Niagara, which had been founded in 1676, and Fort Frontenac, now Kingston, which had been founded in 1673. They descended on the settlement of Lachine, south of Montreal, wiped it out of existence, and carried off nearly a hundred captives, many of whom died at the stake. Most history books call the French invasions of the Iroquois lands "punitive expeditions," while the retaliation by the Indians is called "the Lachine massacre."

a foolish enterprise

Denonville also sent an expedition to attack the English posts in Hudson Bay, led by Pierre le Moyne d'Iberville, later to be the most famous guerrilla leader of his time. But it was a foolish enterprise, risking war with England at a time when the two countries were at peace. Peace was patched up for the time being by a delegation sent to London, but William of Orange arrived in London soon afterwards, and war with Louis XIV became inevitable.

New France now faced its gravest danger since the time of Champlain. In this emergency Frontenac was sent out again as governor. The Iroquois continued to raid the St. Lawrence Valley and to disrupt the fur trade until Frontenac, still a vigorous military leader at the age of 74, destroyed the Onondaga and Oneida villages in 1696, and the Iroquois sued for peace.

Despite the demands of war and Iroquois raids, during Frontenac's governorship the push westward continued. The *coureurs de bois* had at last been taken back into official favour, and had been sent to man the first fort built on the St. Clair River near what is now Sarnia. Detroit was founded in 1701 and remained part of Canada until 1796, when it was handed over to the United States by treaty.

At this point the distinction between the *coureur* and the official explorer begins to fade. It became easy to get commissions, and a chain of French forts—small log stockades, most of them, manned by perhaps half a dozen muskets—spread westward through Ontario, Manitoba, Saskatchewan and the Dakotas.

dreaming of the silk trade

Incredible as it may seem, the French at this time and for another forty years still hoped to reach China overland from Montreal. Lured westward by reports of a nation that built houses, had pet cats, and rode horses, they brought back three captive children from the west who were said to have come from this nation. Taken to Montreal, the children obliged them by playing horse and by petting the kittens which they said were "just like the ones at home."

Still dreaming of the silk trade two centuries after Cartier, the French persuaded themselves that the horses and cats must have come from China or some other civilized nation of Asia, only a short journey west of the prairies. The truth, of course, was that the Mexicans had cats, and had owned Spanish horses for some two hundred years. The animals had gradually moved northward by barter and theft, passing from tribe to tribe until they reached the Great Plains.

The most prominent exploring family was the La Vérendryes. Like so many other pioneers of the

D'Iberville

The most ruthless and persistent scourge in France's campaigns to stop English expansion, Pierre Le Moyne D'Iberville saw his first action at 21 against the HBC fur forts on Hudson Bay in 1682. For fifteen years, he fought a see-saw battle for the northern fur empire before the Treaty of Ryswick divided the East Main in 1697. D'Iberville's next battleground was Newfoundland. After four bloody months, only two of 38 settlements were still standing. For D'Iberville war was a good business. A shrewd profiteer, he was as much a soldier of fortune for himself as for the crown. After firming France's tenuous claim to the Louisiana territory, he attacked British holdings in the Caribbean, but died after the victory of an unknown disease in Cuba, aged 45. A probe into his business activities showed he had illegally skimmed off 112,000 *livres* in one campaign.

Pierre Le Moyne D'Iberville
Soldier of Fortune

D'Iberville's 1697 capture of York Fort followed a brilliant victory over three British men-of-war. The 44-gun Pelican *was abandoned after sending two of the 124-gun armada to the bottom.*

99

Pierre Gaultier, better known as La Vérendrye, was the first systematic explorer of the prairies. His search for a route to the "Western Sea" was frustrated by his lack of money and the demands of his Montreal backers. He himself only reached the western shore of Lake Winnipeg, but in 1743, his sons (right) sighted the foothills.

west, they came from Trois-Rivières. The father, Pierre, had served in the colonial army. After his discharge, he began fur trading and was soon appointed commandant of a small fort on Lake Nipigon. Moving west, he commanded the post founded by Daniel Dulhut at Thunder Bay, and from this fort he began the series of explorations that ended in his sons' reaching the Rockies.

The Indians had told him about Lake Winnipeg, and he understood them to say that out of it flowed a great river in a westerly direction. This was quite wrong, of course, but he reported it back to Quebec, and the governor was so excited by the news that he wrote a dispatch to France predicting that La Vérendrye would soon reach "the western sea, in which, to all appearances, that great river discharges." On the strength of this wild hope La Vérendrye was given a trading monopoly of the Lake Winnipeg region.

La Vérendrye sent his nephew and one of his sons to build a fort on Rainy Lake, while he himself remained at Lake of the Woods. In 1734, his second son, Pierre, was put in charge of a new post on the Red River, and in the autumn of 1738, La Vérendrye and his two sons, Louis-Joseph and François, founded Portage La Prairie on the Assiniboine River. In 1742 and 1743, Louis-Joseph and François made the two-year journey to the west on which they reported a great range of snow-capped peaks along the western horizon.

The dream of reaching China came to an end with the discovery of this formidable barrier, but the explorations continued up and down the Saskatchewan River.

With the La Vérendryes, the French exploring effort not only reached its peak but was also coming to an end. It became harder and harder to raise the money for such work. The government could provide none at all, and the Montreal merchants who had financed the family did not consider the returns big enough. The Hudson's Bay Company, in fact, was winning the struggle for the west.

Anthony Henday strides into the winter camp of the Alberta Blackfoot in 1754 – the first white man to reach the foot-hills of the Rockies. He was hired by the HBC to woo the Indians back to trading with the company, and in that sense his mission was a failure: the French *coureurs*, he said, had already established a trading network in the area. Henday made his year-long trek in the company of a band of Cree and a woman he called his "food-gatherer, cook and bed-fellow." When Henday's journal was sent to London, every mention of her was cut: the company did not approve of such goings-on.

ETAT RAISONNÉ

DES PROVISIONS

PLUS NECESSAIRES

Quand il s'agit de donner commencement a
des Colonnies estrangeres.

S I une fois on formoit
un dessein arresté d'-
établir des Colonnies
en Canada, ou en qu'-
elqu'autre partie de
l'Amerique, auec les vûes, et sur le pied
qu'elles ont été cy-deuant proposées, La

LA COCHONNERIE

OU

CALCUL ESTIMATIF.

pour connoitre jusqu'ou peut aller la produ.
d'une Truie, pendant dix années de temps

O N supose qu'une tru-
ie, la seconde année
de son âge, porte une
ventrée de six cochons
mâles et femelles, do.
nous ne compterons que les femelles, at=

The first guides for emigrants to the French colonies in North America were published in the early-1700s with ornate title pages, such as the ones above. Etat Raisonné is a list of what the would-be colonist should bring along.

La Cochonnerie, or how to set up a pig farm in ten years — starting with one sow, the author estimated the first year's litter at six piglets, and from there nature took its course. By 1700, Canada was agriculturally self-sufficient.

CHAPTER NINE

The Intendant's Château and the Habitant's Farm

With regard to the farmers who devote their energies assiduously to the land, they live very respectably and are in an incomparably happier position than those who in France are called the good peasants.

Letter from Duchesneau to Colbert, 1679

Despite some romantic pictures of early eighteenth-century life, hard work and worries dominated the everyday lives of nearly everyone. From sun-up to sunset, farmers and their wives and children tended their fields and flocks, knowing that each lost row of crops and head of livestock meant a loss of livelihood. Craftsmen and merchants often waited idly while supply ships carrying iron, cloth, spices, salt, brandy and wine made their way across the Atlantic. Once docked, the cargo would be picked over by the governor's or intendant's men or the clergy before reaching the workers.

Everyone had his or her place in society and passed it on to the next, and the next, generation. Still, out of reach of the authorities, people did pretty well what they pleased. After all, most communities had their own very effective methods of dealing with reprobates. But once in the hands of the magistrates, justice was usually meted out according to what the defendent could afford.

The penalty for blasphemy in Quebec in 1636 was a fine which was doubled with every offence until the fifth. If the swearing continued, the foul-mouthed citizen could be sent to the pillory, have his lower lip cut off, or have his tongue cut out. Murder and rape were punishable by hanging, as was the case with Jacques Pourpoint in 1686. He was accused of deserting his platoon and raping the wife of a local resident. His sentence: "to be hanged and strangled, until death results, on a gibbet which will be erected in the lower town, having first been led naked in his shirt, a burning torch in his hand, before the main door of the parish church, there to ask pardon of God for the said crimes." To set a public example, the head of the dead man was to be severed from the body and placed atop a stake planted at a crossroads, "there to remain as long as it holds together".

Nevertheless, there was some resistance to these harsh and unusual punishments. On at least one occasion, the carpenters at Quebec were forced at gunpoint to build a gallows; on another, drovers refused to drag corpses of executed criminals through the streets, as the courts ordered. At Trinity in Newfoundland, a mob rescued a fisherman from the whipping post and tried to tear down the courthouse where he was sentenced.

Civil ordinances governed almost every aspect of daily life in New France. Townspeople were required by law to construct latrines and privvies "to avoid the infection and stink that the filth produces when it is in the street." No one was allowed to carry an open flame or to smoke in the streets—

Hot-headed young officers of the regiment often drew swords when their honour – or a lady's – was in question. The histories of many prominent Quebec and Montreal families are peppered with details of duels over gambling debts, love triangles and petty jealousies.

Witchcraft

Thirty years before the wave of witchcraft trials rocked Salem, Massachusetts in New England, a Montreal tribunal convicted René Besnard of casting a spell of impotence over his former-lover's husband – "by incantation over a thrice-knotted string." Besnard was imprisoned, and three years later Bishop Laval annulled the still-barren marriage of Pierre Gadois and Marie Pontonnier on grounds of "permanent impotence caused by witchcraft." Marie remarried two months later; Pierre waited five years. His second wife, Jeanne Besnard (no relation to the culprit), eventually bore him 12 children, the last a set of twins.

Transportation depended almost completely on lakes and rivers. From four to six months each year, the waters were not navigable and became highways of ice. From spring breakup, flat-bottom boats were guided by shore-lines down rapids.

"on pain of corporal punishment." Streets had to be swept and kept clear of refuse by property owners. And in case of fire, neighbors were summoned by ringing church bells to fill their buckets and rush to the scene of the disaster.

While governors and magistrates saw to it that the public stayed within the limits of the law, priests and bishops worried about the moral character of the colonists. Since church and state usually worked hand-in-glove, the private lives of villagers were always under scrutiny. A decree of 1707 forbade Montrealers from "taking home loose women." In 1710, Intendant Antoine-Denis Raudot prohibited the *habitants* of Lachine "to leave church during the sermon, or to chat, flirt, or indulge in any form of immodest conduct during divine service."

Quebec bishops Laval and St. Vallier ordered priests to refuse absolution and Holy Communion to "those women who wear their ostentation even in our churches . . . exposing to the view scandalous expanses of arm, shoulders and bosom, contenting themselves by veiling them in transparent stuff, which very often only lends lustre to their shameful nakedness."

Inns and taverns were operated by permit only, and licenses specified that no scandals, drunkeness, blasphemy or gambling would be tolerated. In 1694, when Jacques de Maureuil planned to stage Moliere's *Tartuffe* for Quebeckers, Bishop St. Vallier decreed that anyone attending the production would be guilty of a mortal sin. The bishop then bribed Governor Frontenac to cancel the play, on the grounds that "these sorts of comedies are not only dangerous, but that they are absolutely bad and criminal."

During forty years of relative peace (1713-1754), broken only by piracy and privateering,

Until the mid-1700s, the only English "towns" in Canada were the fur posts on Hudson Bay. All other settlements were French. When the English assault on Acadia began, Halifax and Fort Lawrence (above) were built, in 1750.

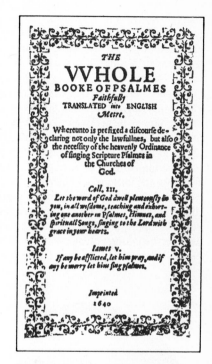

Canadian colonies both French and English, flourished. The population of Quebec expanded from twenty to fifty thousand, and the English population of Newfoundland from two to six thousand. The population of Nova Scotia, mainly by infiltration from New England, but also by natural increase among Acadian farmers, rose from fifteen hundred to fourteen thousand. Halifax was founded in 1749 by a strong garrison of English troops under Edward Cornwallis, as the English "answer" to Louisbourg.

Canadian life in this period took on a sense of permanence. The people were no longer transients in a strange land or pioneers seeking a place in the wilderness, but third and fourth generation Canadians, Nova Scotians, or Newfoundlanders. Though remaining "citizens" of France or Britain, as the case might be, they were now at home in the new land, and developing a culture of their own.

Writing in 1719, one of the merchants of Quebec described the *Canadiens* in a letter to France:

. . . the people living here have had, in this colony, great great grandparents, great grandparents, grandparents, fathers . . . they have their own families, of which the greater number are quite large; they were the first to contribute to the establishment of the colony . . . cultivated its lands, built its churches, erected its crosses, maintained its religion, constructed its fine buildings, helped fortify its towns, and fought successfully against the Indians as well as against the other enemies of the State . . . .

In Acadia it was French peasant culture, simple, solid, founded on a long tradition of manual skills. Every wife must spin and weave, every husband work with wood and stone. The people were wholly self-sufficient, living on reclaimed salt marshes where their every need was supplied by

Music in both French and English settlements was either profane or sacred. Of the first kind, most was based on Old World love songs, bawdy ballads and boisterous sea shanties. Music in the churches in general was relatively new. In the English Protestant churches, The Whole Booke of Psalmes (the first book printed in English America) included a discourse on the lawfulness of singing. In Quebec, the music of Father Charles-Amador Martin (Canada's first composer) "raised greatly the level of performance of religious ceremonies."

A Family Dynasty

Like father, like sons – it was the way most dynasties were built, and the Vaudreuils were no different. When father Philippe de Rigaud de Vaudreuil arrived in Canada, he was 44, a career officer who had been a member of the king's elite Musketeers. Rather than spend the rest of his life as a minor officer, he accepted the post of commander of the troops in Canada, and in 1703 was named governor. A military man, not an administrator, he managed, however, to survive the intrigues of power-hungry men, and remained governor for 22 years. His six sons followed their father's career: Louis-Philippe joined the navy; Philippe-Antoine the infantry; Jean the Musketeers; Pierre, François and Joseph were governors.

Philippe de Rigaud de Vaudreuil – the father.

Pierre – the last governor of New France.

Louis-Philippe – naval lieutenant-general.

the soil. With simple tools such as hand shovels they performed great engineering feats, building the system of dikes that kept back the enormous Fundy tides and provide protection for tens of thousands of fertile acres below sea-level. There was practically no government in Acadia. None was needed. The only authority was the village priest, sole representative of the "outside."

In Newfoundland and coastal Nova Scotia it was West-Country English fishing culture. Most people there lived in houses little better than huts standing on bare rock to be as near as possible to the great fishing grounds. Flakes and fish stores were the more substantial structures of those fishing outposts, and as time passed more and more of the people built winter houses, not at the fishing rooms, but in the recesses of the bays, protected from seas and gales, close to a supply of firewood. Thus they became seasonal migrants, a new feature of life in the new world.

unlike Europe.

Unlike the Atlantic communities, Quebec developed a way of life distinctly different from anything in Europe, strongly influenced by the Indians. Even between Quebec and Montreal, the canoe remained the principal means of communication until the first crude road between the two towns was opened in 1734. Trapping, hunting and long wilderness journeys were all a regular part of life in Canada, as they had not been in Europe since the close of the Bronze Age. In winter, everyone travelled on snowshoes. Indian dress, somewhat modified, had become the working garb of the colony, replacing the eighteenth-century costumes of France for all except "society." French institutions were grafted on to a way of life not drastically changed from that of the Iroquoian farmers of Cartier's time. Even the crops were largely of Indian origin.

Winter, by now, was no terror, but a season for sport. The Jesuit Charlevoix, describing life at Quebec in 1720, talks of sledge trips and skating parties. Huge fur muffs were in fashion for the ladies, and they wore masks to protect their faces from the cold. Hunting was a favourite sport, but also a serious occupation. Some gentlemen, says Charlevoix, did nothing else. There was no great wealth but no serious poverty either. Bread, fish and meat were all plentiful and cheap.

building forever

The earliest houses at Quebec were half-timbered with exposed beams, the spaces between the beams filled with a mixture of rubble and mortar, but these soon gave place to large, oblong, two-storied structures, sometimes with hipped roofs and sometimes with gables. Along the St. Lawrence, both timber and limestone were plentiful, and the latter when first quarried can be cut into blocks with an ordinary wood saw. Exposure later hardens it into a stone that will last for centuries. Timber houses like those of the first pioneers would have been easier, but these people were building, as they thought, forever.

The colonial habitations of Quebec were built like forts, with walls two to four feet thick, an inner layer of stone, then a layer of rubble, then an outer layer of stone covered with stucco and whitewash. This gave good insulation, was easy to maintain, and offered a stout defence against raids. Roofs were heavy-beamed and cedar-shingled. A special feature of these early houses was the "great hall" occupying the whole of the ground floor. Like the halls of medieval castles, these rooms served for everything except sleeping (and sometimes for that too). They combined the functions of kitchen, workroom and sitting room, and were big enough to entertain a whole settlement at a wedding or a wake. They had huge fireplaces at

BARBIER COIFFEUR au 17ᵉ S.
d'ap. Ab. Bosse

Dictated by whims and vanities of European monarchs, long hair—one's own or full wigs—came into vogue in the mid-1600s and stayed for over a century. Beards were considered "barbarian" among the barber's wealthy, modish clientele. We know that Henri Lamarre, a barber in Quebec, almost went bankrupt when a nervous disorder forced him to close down his business in 1736.

Marie-Elisabeth Bégon left to live in France after her husband, Claude-Michel (opposite), died in 1748. An avid letter writer, she kept up with the daily life, gossip, scandals and goings-on in Canada through correspondence with relatives. The letters, found nearly 200 years later in Paris, candidly detail the high-living, decadent days of Intendant François Bigot.

both ends, the chimneys sometimes double-flued for stoves downstairs and fireplaces upstairs.

Wood was in limitless supply and went up the chimneys in vast quantities. A letter written in 1644 by Marie de l'Incarnation to her son reports that in the convent's four fireplaces they burned annually 175 cords of wood (22,400 cubic feet). But fireplaces alone could not heat a house properly in the Canadian winter–not to mention the nuisance of doing all the cooking in hanging pots. By 1668, the first iron stoves were installed at Quebec, and the Ursulines were among the first to welcome the innovation, long before such new-fangled inventions had become popular in France.

Most of the furniture in early colonial Canada was made by the habitants themselves or by skilled woodworkers among the colonists, some of whom specialized in cabinetmaking and wood-carving. Early Quebec furniture was not merely functional but often highly finished and elaborately decorated, with turned and carved legs for tables and chairs, imitating the styles then popular in Europe. All of it, however, was made in native wood. The fashion for imported wood and faithful copies of the European styles did not begin until a century later.

If everyday life for most colonists in the early 1700s was frugal and unadorned, matters were quite different at the intendant's palace. French Court fashions were in vogue–long, hooped skirts with petticoats and tight bodices for women; coats, waistcoats, breeches and stockings for men. Ruffles and lace circled the cuffs and neckline.

Gentlemen went about their appointed business, mostly poking their noses into family holdings or affairs of the army or government. Dining and partying were year-round attractions, and sometimes the *soirées* went on into the dawn. Marie-Elizabeth Bégon, wife of the governor of Trois-Rivières, described one in a letter written around 1750:

There was a great deal of drinking at M. de Lantanac's dinner last evening. Everybody had difficulty dancing the minuet; then it was agreed that they should all go to eat at Deschambault's. Again they drank a great deal of wine, five bottles between M. de Noyan and Saint-Luc, who, as you can imagine, passed out.

What shocked Madame Bégon most was Monsieur de Noyan falling to the floor while dancing the minuet, losing his wig, and making a fool of himself–and in front of the English visitors, yet!

It is fortunate for all those who indulge in dancing that they have two days of rest, for I believe they would die otherwise. They left the ball this morning at six o'clock.

Gambling and loose living were the talk of the town in Quebec in the last days of New France. The intendant, François Bigot, gave lavish dinner parties, flitted from one mistress to another, and turned his château into a veritable Monte Carlo. His losses at the gaming table were estimated at 204,000 *livres* (a *large* fortune in the day), most of it taxpayers' money.

When the Chevalier de Lévis wooed away Bigot's mistress, Madame Pénissault, the intendant found swift consolation in the affections of Madame Péan. The clergy condemned such scandals, of course, as they did the vices of the working man. But it was harder to dictate morals and manners to those who held the balance of power.

Such was life on the eve of the fall of New France: hard times, unemployment and food shortages for the farmer and labourer; extravagance, gaiety and well-stocked tables for the elite. As the Marquis de Montcalm described it: "High life in spite of the miseries and impending loss of the colony has been most active in Quebec. There have never been so many balls and so much gambling."

Captain Claude-Michel Bégon was billetted at the house of Etienne Rocbert when he fell in love with the Montreal storekeeper's daughter, Marie-Elisabeth (opposite). Though his family opposed a liaison with such a low-born girl, the two eloped in classic story-book fashion. Married in 1718, he remained in the army until appointed governor of Trois-Rivières in 1743.

The Death of a General

James Wolfe was only 32 years old when he was called to plan and execute the Quebec campaign. Rash, arrogant, constantly bickering with his senior officers, military historians have gone as far as calling him "a second-rate commander." Quebec was his first command. After two months of waiting, and one disastrous, bloody assault, he risked a daring advance up to the Plains of Abraham, where he fell in the charge.

The DEATH of the Great WOLF.

"We have overcome all Opposition!" exclaimed the Messengers. "I'm satisfied." said the Dying Hero, & Expired in the Moment of Victory.

To Benj.ⁿ West Esq.ʳ President of the Royal Academy, this attempt to Emulate the Beauties of his unequall'd Picture of the Death of Gen.ˡ Wolfe, is most respectfully submitted, by the Author.

This 1795 caricature of Benjamin West's painting (opposite) suggests that not everyone was taken in by the popular legends circulated about Wolfe. Nor does the author of the lampoon show any great reverence for Benjamin West's fantastical painting.

Only the officer with the flag was in the group of four men at Wolfe's side on the morning of September 13, 1759. All the others in Benjamin West's "immortal" painting were elsewhere. When the artist asked James Murray if he wanted to be included (for a fee), Murray replied, "No, no! I was not by."

A View of the Landing the New England Forces in y̆ Expedition against CAPE BRETON 1745.

"When after a Siege of 40 days the Town and Fortress of LOUISBOURG and the important Territories thereto belonging were recover'd to the British Empire. The brave & Active Commodore Warren, since made Knight of the Bath & Vice Admiral of y̆ White commanded the British Squadron in this glorious Expedition, the Hon. Will.ᵐ Pepperell Esq.ʳ since Knighted went a Voluntier & Commanded the New England Men who bravely offer'd their service and went ──── ── ── ate Soldiers in this hazardous but very glorious Enterprize.

Louisbourg, touted by France's military engineers as "the Gibraltar of America," was attacked by Colonel Pepperell's New England forces in May 1745. During the month-long siege, British batteries pounded the citadel day and night. On June 26, the beleagured inhabitants and soldiers petitioned Governor Du Chambon to surrender. Supposedly invulnerable, the fortress had several flaws: it was surrounded by hills ideal for enemy cannon, and nearby coves made landing quite simple. Cape Breton's damp climate didn't help: slow in setting, the lime-mortar walls crumbled from the shock of Louisbourg's own cannon.

CHAPTER TEN

From Louisbourg to Quebec

*Tell M. de Vaudreuil I have come to take
Canada and I will take nothing less.*

Jeffrey Amherst to Louis-Antoine de Bougainville,
Montreal, September 7, 1760

George Washington, some twenty years later to become the "Father of his Country," fired the shot that started the war that brought New France to an end. French North America covered a vast territory, from Newfoundland to the prairies, northward almost to Hudson Bay, and southward through the Ohio and Mississippi to Louisiana. But it was held by a mere handful of colonists. In its closing years New France, with a population of about sixty thousand, was pitted against British North America with a population of over a million.

The co-existence of the two North American empires had always been uneasy, and perhaps the final war was inevitable. It started when Virginia decided to stake a claim on the Ohio, and in 1755, Washington leading a detachment of Virginian troops, attacked a party of thirty Canadians. Seven or eight were killed and the rest retreated. But Washington's Indian allies intercepted them and killed and scalped their commander. Washington then turned back to the east and entrenched his raiders at a place he named "Fort Necessity," where he was besieged and forced to sign articles of capitulation, promising that Virginia would not build another fort on the Ohio for a year.

But the war was on. That winter a thousand British regulars landed in Virginia under General Braddock. He was defeated and killed in his first encounter with the French, and other generals, no better than he, were sent to replace him.

Meanwhile, the British troops from Halifax were burning the Acadian farms and expelling their owners, scattering the French-speaking peasants in small groups through the English colonies all the way to the Gulf of Mexico. A few went to France, others to Cape Breton, western Newfoundland, Prince Edward Island, Quebec and Labrador. After many years, some of them returned and settled once more on the burnt-out farms where they had been born.

In Acadia, the oath of allegiance was not really the issue but the excuse for the expulsion. Most French colonials were willing to swear allegiance to the conqueror when pressed. Except for the garrison at Placentia which was moved to Cape Breton, French settlers in Newfoundland had stayed in their settlements and become British subjects after Newfoundland was confirmed to Britain by the Treaty of Utrecht. Captain Taverner, sent along the coast to administer the oath of loyalty, encountered little opposition anywhere.

The Acadians were given no choice. They were simply rounded up and shipped off under armed guard. If they offered to swear allegiance to Britain, they were told they should have done that a

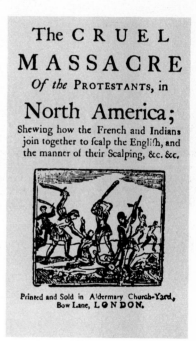

The CRUEL
MASSACRE
Of the PROTESTANTS, in
North America;
Shewing how the French and Indians join together to scalp the English, and the manner of their Scalping, &c. &c.

Printed and Sold in Aldermary Church-Yard,
Bow Lane, LONDON.

*Revenge for Louisbourg (opposite)
was one of the motives for raids
by the French and their Iroquois
allies on tiny New England towns.
From Fort Saint-Frédéric on Lake
Champlain, they moved south as far
as Deerfield, Mass., leaving a
trail of fire and blood behind.*

Twenty-five years before George Washington (mounted) fought against England in the war of independence, he was fighting the French. With all the pretention of a Virginia slave-owner, he claimed the entire Ohio River territory for his land company. In 1754, he surrendered to the French, but the war was on.

114

generation before. There was some military excuse (as well as precedent) for the expulsion. The Acadians were seen as a potential fifth column of dangerous size in a province very thinly held by English troops, and a few of them were, indeed, fighting against the English.

Montcalm "the invincible"

In 1755, the British announced a blockade of New France and sent a fleet to enforce it. In coastal waters they met a French fleet of eighteen vessels carrying three thousand men. The French were totally out-gunned by the British, and, according to the rules of the game, the war for Canada should have ended right there with the capture of the French troopships. As it turned out, the British captured only two ships. Fifteen escaped in the fog and got up the St. Lawrence to Quebec; the other made its way to Louisbourg.

The next year, the Marquis de Montcalm with two regiments of reinforcements reached Canada before the British, simply by sailing before the Royal Navy was ready to leave port. He promptly began a campaign of border warfare against New England, and soon gained a reputation as "invincible" – not so much because he was a general, but because his opponents consistently managed to lead superior forces to disaster.

Montcalm's successes grew from year to year. In 1758, he won his third great victory when a British army of fifteen thousand was sent against a strongly fortified position that he held with three thousand men. For some reason, the British broke rank and fled in disorder. The British, by now, had built Montcalm into a military genius, the most famous French general in the world.

As the war dragged on, with the British losing most of the battles, they began, through sheer necessity, to send out leaders of some ability. Jeffrey Amherst was put in charge of all British troops in

North America, and James Wolfe, a man of great spirit determined to win glory if possible, was sent to attack Quebec.

Amherst laid siege to Louisbourg, the only French base on the Atlantic, which the British had been attempting to blockade with varying success since 1755. There were about six thousand men in the fortress and fewer than ten warships in port, only two of them fully armed. The force that Amherst brought against it numbered twenty-seven thousand, supported by thirty-five to forty warships. He made a landing in Gabarouse Bay, well out of reach of the French guns, while the fortress itself was heavily bombarded by his ships. Rather surprisingly, considering the hopelessness of their situation, the French garrison held out for seven weeks. They surrendered on July 26, 1758, but they had resisted long enough to make the amphibious assault on Quebec planned for that year impossible.

Wolfe was not pleased

Wolfe was not pleased. He thought Amherst should have carried Louisbourg by storm if necessary, considering his numerical advantage. Irate, he sailed up the St. Lawrence, to make "an end of the French colony in North America in one campaign."

But Amherst was prudent where Wolfe was impetuous. Louisbourg had been taken with scarcely any loss to the British, and its capture ended the French naval threat in the western Atlantic, permitting the British to deploy troops elsewhere.

Despite the fall of Louisbourg, the French managed to get a supply fleet up the St. Lawrence the following year. The eighteen French ships arrived in the nick of time, the Royal Navy, Wolfe and nine thousand British troops right behind them. Again, the British had thrown away the chance for a cheap victory. Had Wolfe sailed a

Ironically, it was an American, not a Canadian, who immortalized the sad tale of Evangeline (above) and the expulsion of the Acadiens *from their New Brunswick and Nova Scotia homes in 1755. In fact, although Henry Wadsworth Longfellow's long (sometimes tedious) poem is on most U.S. high school reading lists, very few Canadians know he ever wrote it, and even fewer have bothered to read it. A bronze statue of Evangeline, cast in Paris by the Canadian sculptor Philippe Hébert, a descendent of Louis (page 63), was unveiled in 1920.*

Of the scores of pictures claiming to be portraits of James Wolfe, George Townshend's watercolour is the only one done from life. He had reddish hair, blue eyes, and must have been somewhat of a ladies' man, as his three engagements and numerous cartoons about him suggest. At the time of his death, he was engaged to Elizabeth Lawson, and wore a miniature cameo portrait of her around his neck into battle.

month earlier, Quebec might have been starved into submission without a fight.

While Wolfe anchored between Quebec and Île d'Orléans, Amherst, with six thousand troops advanced by way of Lake Champlain. Had these forces joined up, they would have numbered fifteen thousand, giving the British an overwhelming numerical advantage. They did not. Amherst stopped to rebuild the abandoned French forts and left the siege of Quebec to Wolfe. A third British force from New England captured the French fort at Niagara. Quebec and Montreal were now the only remaining centres of resistance. Wolfe captured Point-Lévis on the bank of the St. Lawrence, just opposite the Quebec citadel, and mounted mortars with which to bombard the town. He then began campaigning up and down the river, landing small parties to skirmish with opposing parties of French, and systematically destroying the houses and farms. Even if Quebec held out, both the town and the surrounding farmlands would be reduced to ruins by the end of the summer.

distress in the valley

It was a summer of great distress for the farmers of the St. Lawrence Valley. Most of the men were organized into militia, either serving in the combined French and New French forces under Montcalm's command at Quebec, or in the two subsidiary forces. The first under Colonel Bougainville was kept on the march up-river from Quebec to prevent the landing from British ships; the other was stationed in the trenches on the Beauport flats at the mouth of the St. Charles River just below Quebec, commanded by the Marquis de Vaudreuil.

Women, children and men too old to fight, living anywhere outside the walls of Quebec, became refugees, their houses, crops and buildings all put to the torch, their livestock driven off for slaughter. Hundreds of them fled to the army camps, while hundreds of others crowded into the town, seeking the charity of friends and relatives or the subsistence of a government ration. So fierce was Wolfe's campaign against the civilian population of New France that they were convinced he would order a massacre if Quebec were carried by assault. Before the final battle, fourteen hundred farms had been burned, and eighty per cent of the buildings in the town were in ruins.

outnumbered two-to-one

But the continuous skirmishing and the outbreak of fever and dysentery were almost disastrous to the British. By late summer, Wolfe's force of nine thousand was reduced to 4,800, the rest being either sick or dead. Amherst's army simply failed to appear, and as the prospect of the freeze-up drew near, Wolfe was faced with the choice of either withdrawing and admitting failure, or else attacking with his tiny army a strongly fortified town that could muster enough men to outnumber him by more than two-to-one.

In desperation, he accepted a plan put forward by his brigadiers by trying a landing above the town at night. He himself chose the spot where the landing was to be made – much closer than the brigadiers intended – at a place where they had to climb a cliff in single file, making retreat completely impossible. They must either win the battle, surrender, or be killed to the last man. If they were discovered before they were ready to fight, defeat would be certain.

The gamble paid off. Although boats carrying the troops were challenged by French lookouts, the troops managed to persuade the challengers that they were French forces slipping downriver to surprise the British. The guard at the top of the defile was overwhelmed without being able to

BRITISH RESENTMENT or the FRENCH fairly COOPT at Louisbourg.

The key to the action in this 1755 piece of English propaganda reads: 1. Britannia attending to the complaints of her injured Americans [*left*] . . . 4. The British Arms eclipsing those of France [*top left*] . . . 6. An English saylor squeezes the Gallic Cock & makes him disgorge the French usurpations in America [*bottom right*] . . . 9. A gang of brave saylors exulting at the starving French coopt up [*top right*] . . . 10. The French overset at Niagara [*top*]. *Astounding!*

The war was not over with the death of Montcalm and the surrender of Quebec four days later. Even then, French forces remained camped within miles, running out of food but determined to retake the city. Among the soldiers were cooks, nurses, camp-followers and other women.

sound the alarm. By dawn Wolfe had four thousand men on the Plains of Abraham, and by nine o'clock he had his entire force of 4,800, supported by cannon, drawn up within a thousand yards of the walls of Quebec.

Even now, by all the rules, they should have been decimated. Within four hours at the most, the French could have mustered a force of nine thousand capable of attacking the British both in the front and in the rear. But Montcalm lost his head. Had he waited long enough to bring in the troops stationed up-river under Bougainville and the battalion under Vaudreuil from Beauport, he could hardly have failed to win the battle. Instead, he attacked at once with a force approximately equal to Wolfe's but far inferior in training.

All the British troops were seasoned veterans of the regular army. Half the French were militia, trained in bush fighting but wholly lacking the tight discipline needed for a frontal attack in a field battle. They fired at much too long range, dropped to the ground to reload, then ran forward again, the lines becoming ragged and the front lines more and more exposed. The British stood and fired in volleys only when ordered, then reloaded, advanced through the smoke, and fired again. In fifteen minutes it was all over, the French were fleeing back inside the walls, Wolfe was dead, and Montcalm was fatally wounded. He lived only long enough to surrender the town.

Quebec was lost

The date was September 13, 1759. Both Vaudreuil's and Bougainville's troops arrived on the battlefield, but they were too late. Quebec was lost. Even now, the French might have regrouped and defeated the British, but instead they fled upriver and didn't stop before they had put a full day's march between themselves and their pursuers. The British moved into Quebec, and the fleet sailed home.

Next spring at the second battle of Quebec, the British were overwhelmed, but when they fled, they retreated within the walls of the town, and were prepared to withstand a siege. A small force of six ships sent from France to the relief of Quebec was captured and burnt in the Gulf of St. Lawrence. By mid-May, the British fleet was within gun range of the besieging French army on the Plains of Abraham, and the French were forced to withdraw up-river.

the coup de grâce

Three British armies then moved toward Montreal for the *coup de grâce*: one by way of Lake Champlain, a second by Lake Ontario, and the third advancing from Quebec. The two thousand French troops, reduced to this remnant by deaths and desertions, did the only sane thing by surrendering without a fight.

After the surrender, the French had the option of staying in Quebec and accepting British rule or leaving for France. Out of a population of about sixty thousand, a small percentage left, mostly merchants with business connections in France. French deserters from the regular army also remained. Many of them were married to Canadian girls and wanted to stay in Canada regardless of the question of sovereignty. Within four years, some were enlisting in a British regiment to fight the Indians on the western border where the New Englanders had stirred up trouble.

The fall of Montreal was not the end of the war in North America. It ended two years later at the battle of St. John's, the last effort of the French to recoup their losses in North America. As the war approached its end, the question of peace arose, and the possibility that Britain might be willing to return Quebec to France, as she had done once before, in exchange for other concessions. Quebec

Livid at the news of Montcalm's blunderous loss of Quebec, Gaston de Lévis, now in command, regrouped his tattered army. A brilliant victory at Sainte-Foy (above) in April 1760, forced the English to retreat to safety inside the walls of Quebec. Lévis very nearly recaptured the city.

119

Paper Heroes

The war for Canada wasn't fought only on battlefields but in campaign headquarters, as well. There generals fired salvos of ridicule at each other. *"If I had power, I'd kill 20 in an hour,"* reads this caricature of Jeffrey Amherst.

Brigadier-General George Townshend was Wolfe's most scurrilous critic, circulating bawdy cartoons of the general in the officers' mess. The one above plays on Wolfe's suspicions that he was surrounded by "stinking spies."

meant nothing to England. The only British really interested in it were a few New England traders. But the Newfoundland fishery was still one of the mainstays of the British economy.

There were now over twelve thousand permanent English inhabitants in Newfoundland, but perhaps even more important from the British point of view were the other twelve thousand floating fishermen who went there for the summer. The combined fishery produced seventy million pounds of fish, dry weight, annually.

without a fight

The British forts in Newfoundland had been emptied to reinforce the armies in Nova Scotia and on the St. Lawrence. St. John's was left with a garrison of sixty-three men; Ferryland, Carbonear and other fortified towns with even fewer. Eight hundred French troops in four warships eluded the British blockade and landed at Bay Bulls, twenty miles south of St. John's, on August 27, 1762. Next day, they took the English capital without a fight. They repaired the fort that faced the harbour, built a new one on Signal Hill, overlooking both the town and the approach from the sea, and sent off detachments that captured Carbonear and Trinity. But the English governor managed to get reinforcements into Placentia and Ferryland in time to save them.

What followed was a text-book battle, won entirely by strategy. Under Colonel William Amherst, the British landed troops (Scots from Nova Scotia, Swiss and German mercenaries from New York) at Torbay, ten miles north of St. John's, then marched them southward through the woods to Quidi Vidi, capturing that little harbour in a short battle.

Three days after the landing, in the dark of night, the English crept up Signal Hill and took the hilltop fort by surprise. They were now in an unas-sailable position overlooking the town, while most of the French troops remained in the sea-level fort almost five hundred feet below them. The French warships, recognizing the inevitable, slipped off at night in the fog, leaving Count d'Haussonville, the French commander, to deal with the English as best he could.

Canada was now in British hands, and its fate seemed secure. In 1763, the Treaty of Paris confirmed this, France keeping only the small islands of Saint-Pierre and Miquelon as a base for her fishing fleet – the last remnant of the great empire that once stretched from Newfoundland to the Rockies and from Hudson Bay to the Gulf of Mexico.

Quebec, even then, was more of an embarrassment than anything else to the British. In came the New England carpetbaggers, a group by no means popular with the home government or the military governor of Quebec. In England there was a brisk debate in favor of giving Quebec back to France and keeping Guadeloupe, a small island in the West Indies.

the sixteenth colony

Canada now became the sixteenth colony in British North America, but its boundaries bore no resemblance to those of New France. It reached only from the Detroit River to the Gaspé, and north only to Lake St. John on the Saguenay.

Nova Scotia included the whole of what had been Acadia, both shores of the Bay of Fundy, the St. John River, and all the land north to the Baie des Chaleurs, with the islands of Cape Breton and St. John (Prince Edward Island). Newfoundland included the Magdalen Islands, Anticosti, the whole of present-day Labrador, and most of what is now the Quebec North Shore.

The rest of Canada was divided between the Indians and the Hudson's Bay Company, which

DRESS.
the most distinguishing mark of a military Genius.

Tongue-in-cheek, the artist behind this lampoon of officers' foppery titled the piece "Dress – the most distinguishing mark of a military genius." In the 1700s, fashion demanded that all men of position wear powdered wigs: long styles for social occasions, bob wigs for less formal events, and shorter campaign wigs for manoeuvres and battle.

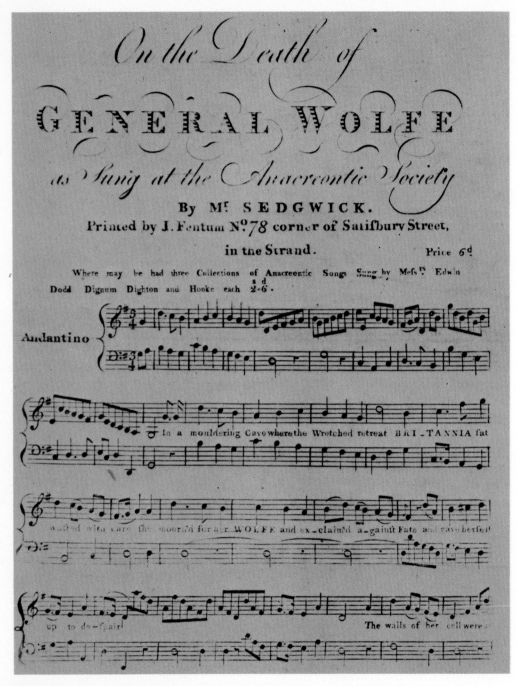

By the time the facts about the fall of New France crossed the Atlantic, both Wolfe and Montcalm were larger-than-life heroes, idolized by poets and composers like Mr. Sedgwick.

claimed a vast territory stretching from Labrador to the Pacific Ocean, not quite reaching southward to the Great Lakes, but dipping far south into the American West. There would be another century of conflict and social turmoil before the borders became reasonably stable.

The future Canada had hardly any English-speaking population in 1760. The thirteen colonies from Maine south to Georgia were still "Britain Overseas," with more than a million colonists. Newfoundland had twelve thousand English-speaking and perhaps two thousand French-speaking inhabitants. Nova Scotia had a total of about twelve thousand, most of them New Englanders who had settled at Annapolis and around Shelburne, in the extreme south. Halifax was still a fortress, with no permanent population. In another twenty years it would become a town of twelve hundred.

sixty thousand habitants

But the Acadians were already returning, and thousands of them would be back before the end of the decade, seeking their ancestral farms along the shores of Fundy and Minas. Nova Scotia's period of growth had just begun. Quebec was a small colony consisting of the river valleys of the Ottawa and the St. Lawrence, sixty thousand people mostly *habitant* farmers, trappers and fur-traders, with a handful of New England businessmen and English-speaking officials working through French-speaking secretaries. The West Coast was not yet explored at all. And then there was Rupert's Land, half a continent inhabited by nomadic Indians and a few dozen fur-traders, most of it unexplored by Europeans, none of whom suspected that this land was a nation in the making.

122

Vain and pompous, Louis-Joseph de Montcalm began talking about the "inevitable defeat" of New France two years after he arrived in Canada. He had no respect for his Canadian soldiers and their guerrilla tactics, and argued about strategy with his superior, Governor Vaudreuil, until his dying breath.

123

Acknowledgements

I wrote this book during the year I was writer in residence at the University of Western Ontario. All the research was done in my own library and in the libraries of the university. I must thank the university for making splendid facilities available to me, and for being very reasonable with its demands on my time.

With few exceptions, the research consisted of reading of well-known primary sources—Whitbourne, Lescarbot, Champlain—and where translation from French sources was involved, the translations are my own.

I have to thank Jean Johnston for turning me on to Marguerite de Roberval and convincing me that Jeanne Mance was the major force in the founding of Montreal. Jean's scholar husband, Stafford Johnston, made me a gift of *The Iroquois Book of Rites*, which I found very illuminating and useful.

Harold Horwood.

Harold Horwood has been a labour organizer, politician, reporter, columnist, editor, freelance writer and novelist. He has travelled extensively in the tropics and the arctic and sailed his own ship to Labrador. An assistant to Premier Smallwood in the campaign that brought Newfoundland into Confederation in 1949 he was Labrador's first representative in the Newfoundland legislature. Among his books are *Newfoundland, Death on the Ice, Voices Underground, Only the Gods Speak and Bartlett, the great Canadian Explorer.* He is the author of numerous magazine articles and number of short stories.

Index

The page numbers in italics refer
to illustrations and captions

127

Picture Credits

We would like to acknowledge the help and co-operation of the directors and staff of the various public institutions and the private firms and individuals who made available paintings, posters, mementoes, collections and albums as well as photographs, and gave us permission to reproduce them. Every effort has been made to identify and credit appropriately the sources of all illustrations used in this book. Any further information will be appreciated and acknowledged in subsequent editions.

The illustrations are listed in the order of their appearance on the page, left to right, top to bottom. Principal sources are credited under their abbreviations:

GA	Glenbow Alberta Institute
GP	Giraudon, Paris
MTL	Metro Toronto Library
NG	National Gallery of Canada
PAC	Public Archives of Canada
ROM	Royal Ontario Museum
WCC-NBM	Webster Canadiana Collection, New Brunswick Museum.

Question: *Who was this man Melech Augustus Hultazob, and why did he call himself "The Prince of Canada" in 1718?*
Answer: *We've done our best but we don't know.*

/1 Château de Ramezay, Montreal /2 City of Bristol Museum and Art Gallery /4 GA /6 PAC /7 Royal Library, Copenhagen, Denmark /8 British Museum /9 ROM; Arctic Institute /10 MTL /11 Bibliothèque Nationale, Paris; PAC C52336 /12 *Ballou's Pictorial Drawing-Room Companion* /13 The British Museum /14 PAC C21115 /15 PAC /16 PAC C3686 /17 PAC C6037 /18 Park and Roche Establishment /19 The New York Public Library; GP /20 British Museum /21 Library of Congress /22 Huntington Library /23 ROM /24 The Ursuline Convent, Quebec /25 GP /26 MTL /27 National Library of Canada /28 Cliche des Museés Nationaux; PAC C1144 /29 PAC C10618 /30 PAC C5538 /31 MTL /32 PAC C28389 /33 ROM /34 Bodleian Library, Oxford; MTL /35 The Tate Gallery, London /36 PAC /37 PAC /38 PAC C1247 /39 WCC-NBM # 2695 /40 American Antiquarian Society, Worcester, Mass. /41 PAC C10486 /42 PAC C16945 /43 PAC /44 WCC-NBM # 3736 /45 MTL /46 Collection Sainte-Anne de Beaupré /47 Collection Sainte-Anne de Beaupré /48 ROM /49 PAC C5325 /50 Bettmann Archive /51 Magdalene College, Cambridge /52 Boston Public Library /53 Paul List Verlag, Muenchen /54 Bettmann Archive /55 GP /57 MTL /58 PAC /59 Bettmann Archive /60 PAC C15372 /61 PAC C13320 /62 PAC C9711 /63 PAC /64 MTL /65 PAC C4816 /66 GA /67 *Illustrated London News* /68 PAC /69 Bibliothèque Nationale, Paris /70 MTL /71 PAC C20127 /72 PAC C11232 /73 PAC C20539 /74 PAC C34204 /75 PAC C4506 /76 PAC C6325 /77 Bibliothèque Nationale, Paris /78 Municipalité de Contrecoeur, Province de Québec /79 NG /80 PAC /81 MTL /82 *Le Monde Illustré* /83 PAC C29486 /84 PAC C2838 /85 WCC-NBM # 1719 /86 PAC C34199 /87 Archives Nationales Du Québec /88 Cliche des Musées Nationaux /89 PAC C17059 /90-91 PAC /92 Paul Mellon Collection, National Gallery of Art, Washington /93 ROM /94 MTL /95 GA /96 Private Collection /97 MTL /98 MTL /99 PAC C26026; PAC C12005 /100 WCC-NBM # 5080 /101 From a painting by Franklin Arbuckle, R.C.A. for the Hudson's Bay Company /102 GP; GP /103 MTL /104 PAC C92746; GP /105 WCC-NBM # 334; Canadian Book of Printing /106 PAC C10145; PAC C10614; PAC C10612 /107 PAC C2937 /108 GP /109 Musée du Québec /110 WCC-NBM #2025 /111 NG /112 PAC /113 John Carter Brown Library, Brown University /114 PAC C8983 /115 Private Collection /116 McCord Museum, Montreal /117 MTL /118 Royal Military College /119 MTL /120 WCC-NBM; WCC-NBM #45; WCC-NBM # 1977 /121 Library of Congress /122 WCC-NBM /123 PAC C4263 /128 WCC-NBM # 745.

1660

Adam Dollard des Ormeaux and small force of defenders decimated at the Long Sault.

1662
French settlement started at Placentia Bay, Nfld.

1663
Louis XIV revokes private charters; New France becomes royal province.

Bishop Laval founds Quebec Seminary (Laval University).

1665
Jean Talon appointed Intendant.

Carignan-Salières regiment arrives to defend New France.

The first "King's Daughters" arrive as brides for settlers.

1666
First census of New France: total population 3,215.

1667
Civil courts established.

1668
First brewery built by Talon at Quebec.

1670
Hudson's Bay Company chartered; Prince Rupert named governor of lands around Hudson and James Bays.

Coal first discovered and mined on Cape Breton.

1671
Marquette establishes mission at Sault Ste. Marie.

1672
Immigration and births bring population of New France to 7,605.

Frontenac arrives as governor.

Fort Frontenac founded at site of Kingston.

Marquette and Jolliet reach Mississippi River.

1678
"Brandy Parliament" approves use of liquor in fur trade.

1679
La Salle launches the *Griffon*, first ship built on Great Lakes.

1680

The "Great Comet" (Halley's) appears in December.

1682
La Salle reaches the mouth of the Mississippi.

Henry Kelsey becomes first white man to visit western Canada.

1683
French force led by Radisson destroys HBC Fort Nelson.

1684
Groseilliers surrenders Fort Bourbon (York Fort) to HBC.

1685
Intendant Jacques de Meulles authorizes "card money" as currency during coin shortage.

Lower Town, Quebec ravaged by fire – all 55 buildings burnt.

1686
D'Iberville seizes HBC forts.

1687
Denonville attacks Senecas and builds Fort Niagara.

1689
Force of 1,500 Iroquois devastates Lachine.

1690
Frontenac wages war on English border settlements.

William Phips and Massachusetts militia capture Port-Royal.

Henry Kelsey sets out from York Fort to explore prairies.

English attempt to take Quebec thwarted by Frontenac.

1691
First commercial water mill built at Pétit Pré near Quebec.

1694
Bishop Saint-Vallier bans performance of Molière's *Tartuffe*.

French force under d'Iberville recaptures Fort Bourbon.

1695
The first sawmill in Acadia built on Nashwaak River.

1697
Treaty of Ryswick returns York Fort to HBC.

1698
Louis Hennepin publishes *A New Discovery of a Vast Country in America*.

1699
Bishop Saint-Vallier opens elementary school at Quebec.